2000-2005 BEST ROCK SONGS

ISBN-10: 0-7390-4235-1
ISBN-13: 978-0-7390-4235-9

THE RISING

Words and Music by
BRUCE SPRINGSTEEN

B(9)
E(9)
B(9)
B♭(9)
E♭(9)
B♭(9)
I've gone,
how far I've gone,
how high I've climbed.
E(9)
B(9)
E(9)
E♭(9)
B♭(9)
E♭(9)
On my back's a six - ty pound stone,
on my shoul-der a half mile
B(9)
To Coda
Chorus:
E
B
B♭(9)
E♭
B♭
of line.
Come on up for the ris - ing.
E
B
E
E♭
B♭
E♭
Come on up, lay your hands in mine.
Come on up for the ris -

B E 1. B
B♭ E♭ B♭
ing._ Come on up_ for the ris - ing to - night._
2. B F♯ B E(9)
B♭ F B♭ E♭(9)
ing to - night._ Li___ li li li li li li li, li li li___
F♯ B E(9) F♯ B
F B♭ E♭(9) F B♭
li li li li li li, li li li___ li li li li li
E(9) F♯ B G♯m
E♭(9) F B♭ Gm
li li, li li li___ li li li li li li.
(Inst. solo ad lib....

E
B
F#
E♭
B♭
F
G#m
E
B
Gm
E♭
B♭
F#
Bridge:
G#m
F
Gm
…end solo) There's spi - rits a - bove__ and be - hind___ me, fac -
E
B
F#
E♭
B♭
F
es gone black, eyes burn - in' bright. May their pre - cious blood__ bind__

G#m Gm
E E♭
B B♭
F# F
me, Lord, as I stand be - fore your fier - y light. Li
li li li li li li li, li li li li li li li li
E(9) E♭(9)
li, li li li li li li li li
D.C. al Coda
li li, li li li li li li li li li.
3. I

Coda
E(9)
E♭(9)
B(9)
B♭(9)
Sky of black - ness and sor - row.
(A dream of life.)
Sky of love, sky
of tears.
Sky of glo - ry and sad - ness.
Sky of mer - cy, sky of fear.
Sky of mem - 'ry and shad-
ows.
Your burn - ing wind fills my arms to - night.

E(9)
E♭(9)
B(9)
B♭(9)
E(9)
E♭(9)
Sky of long - ing and emp - ti - ness.
(A dream of life.)
Sky of full - ness, sky of
B(9)
B♭(9)
Chorus:
E
E♭
B
B♭
bless - ed life.
Come on up for the ris - ing.
E
E♭
B
B♭
E
E♭
Come on up, lay your hands in mine.
Come on up for the ris -
B
B♭
E
E♭
B
B♭
ing.
Come on up for the ris - ing to - night.
Li

Verse 2:
Left the house this morning,
Bells ringing filled the air.
Wearin' the cross of my callin'.
On wheels of fire I come rollin' down here.
(To Chorus:)

Verse 3:
I see you, Mary, in the garden,
In the garden of a thousand sighs.
There's holy pictures of our children,
Dancin' in a sky filled with light.
May I feel your arms around me,
May I feel your blood mixed with mine.
A dream of life comes to me,
Like a catfish dancin' on the end of my line.
Sky of blackness and sorrow... etc.
(To Coda)

ADDICTED

Gtr. tuned down 1/2 step:
⑥ = E♭ ③ = G♭
⑤ = A♭ ② = B♭
④ = D♭ ① = E♭

Words and Music by
CHARLES-ANDRE COMEAU,
JEAN-FRANCOIS STINCO, PIERRE BOUVIER,
SEBASTIEN LEFEBVRE, DAVID DESROSIERS
and ARNOLD DAVID LANNI

Moderately ♩. = 94

Guitar → D
Piano → D♭

mf

G G♭ A A♭ D D♭ G G♭ A A♭

Verse:

D D♭ G G♭

1. I heard you're do - ing o - kay, but I want you to know I'm a
2. Since the day I met you and af - ter all we've been through, still a

D D♭

dick. I'm ad - dict - ed to you. I can't pre - tend I don't care
dick. I'm ad - dict - ed to you. I think you know that it's true.

G
G♭
when you don't think a-bout me.
I'd run a thou-sand miles to get you.
Do you think I de-serve this? I
1.
To Next Strain (To Chorus:)
2.
Em D/F♯ G A Em D/F♯
E♭m D♭/F G♭ A♭ N.C. E♭m D♭/F
tried to make you hap-py, but you left an-y way. I'm tried to make you hap-py. I did
G A E G A
G♭ A♭ E♭ G♭ A♭ N.C.
all that I could just to keep you, but you left an-y-way. I'm
Chorus:
D G D A
D♭ G♭ D♭ A♭
try-ing to for-get that I'm ad-dict-ed to you, but I

D
D♭
G
G♭
D
D♭
A
A♭
want it and I need it. I'm ad - dict - ed to you. Now it's
Em7
E♭m7
A
A♭
Em7
E♭m7
o - ver, can't for - get what you said. And I nev - er wan - na
A
A♭
N.C.
1.
G
G♭
A
A♭
D
D♭
do this a - gain. Heart - break - er, heart - break - er,
G
G♭
A
A♭
D
D♭
G
G♭
A
A♭
heart - break - er.

2.
G D/F# Em7 D G D/F#
G♭ D♭/F E♭m7 D♭ G♭ D♭/F
break - er,
heart - break - er.
Bridge:
Em7 A7sus G D/F# Em7 D
E♭m7 A♭7sus G♭ D♭/F E♭m7 D♭
How long will I be wait - ing?
G D/F# Em7 A7sus G D/F#
G♭ D♭/F E♭m7 A♭7sus G♭ D♭/F
Un - til the end of time. I don't know why
Em7 D Em7 D/F# G A
E♭m7 D♭ E♭m7 D♭/F G♭ A♭
I'm still wait - ing. I can't make you mine.

G/B
Gb/Bb
A/C#
Ab/C
Em7
Ebm7
D/F#
Db/F
G
Gb
A
Ab
I'm
Chorus:
D
Db
try - ing__ to for - get that__ I'm ad - dict - ed__ to you, but I
want it__ and I need it.__ I'm ad - dict - ed__ to you. I'm
try - ing__ to for-get that__ I'm ad - dict - ed__ to you, but I want it__ and I need it.__ I'm ad-

G D A Em7 A
G♭ D♭ A♭ E♭m7 A♭
dict - ed to you. Now it's o - ver, can't for - get what you said. And I
Em7 A G A
E♭m7 A♭ G♭ A♭
nev - er wan-na do this a - gain. Heart - break - er, heart -
D G A D
D♭ G♭ A♭ D♭
break - er. I'm ad - dict - ed to you, heart - break - er. I'm ad -
1. 2.
G A G A D
G♭ A♭ G♭ A♭ D♭
dict - ed to you, heart - dict - ed to you, heart - break - er.
rit.

AMERICAN IDIOT

Words by
BILLIE JOE

Music by
GREEN DAY

Verses 1 & 2:
N.C.
Ab5
Db5
Gb5
1. Don't want to be an A - mer - i - can id - i - ot.
2. Well, may - be I am the f** - got A - mer - i - ca.
Db5
Ab5
Gb5
N.C.
Don't want a na - tion un - der the new me - di - a.
I'm not a part of a red - neck a - gen - da.
Ab5
Db5
Gb5
Db5
Ab5
N.C.
Hey, can you hear the sound
Now ev - 'ry - bod - y, do
Ab5
Db5
Gb5
Db5
Ab5
Gb5
of hys - ter - i - a?
the prop - a - gan - da,

N.C.
Ab5
Db5
Gb5
The sub - lim - i - nal mind - f**k A - mer - i - ca.
and sing a - long to the age of par - a - noi - a.
Chorus:
Db5
Ab5
Db
1.2.4. Wel - come to a new kind of ten - sion
3. (Gtr. solo…
Ab
Eb
all a - cross the a - li - en - a - tion, where ev - 'ry - thing is - n't meant
Ab
to be o - kay.

D♭
A♭
Tel - e - vi - sion dreams of to - mor - row, we're not the ones
who're meant to fol - low, for that's e - nough to ar - gue.
E♭
To Coda ⊕
1.
N.C.
A♭5
D♭5
G♭5
(drums only)
D♭5
A♭5
G♭5
A♭5
D♭5
G♭5
D♭5
A♭5

2.
N.C.
Ab5
Db5
Gb5
(drums)
Db5
Ab5
Gb5
Ab5
Db5
Gb5
Db5
Ab5
Db5
Gb5
Db5
Ab5
Gb5
Ab5
Db5
Gb5
Db5
Ab5
D.S. 𝄋

3.
Ab5
Db5
Gb5
...end solo)
mp
Verse 3:
3. Don't want to be an A - mer - i - can id - i - ot,
one na - tion con - trolled by the me - di - a.
In - for - ma - tion age of hys - ter - i - a
N.C.
is call - ing out to id - i - ot A - mer - i - ca.
D.S. % al Coda

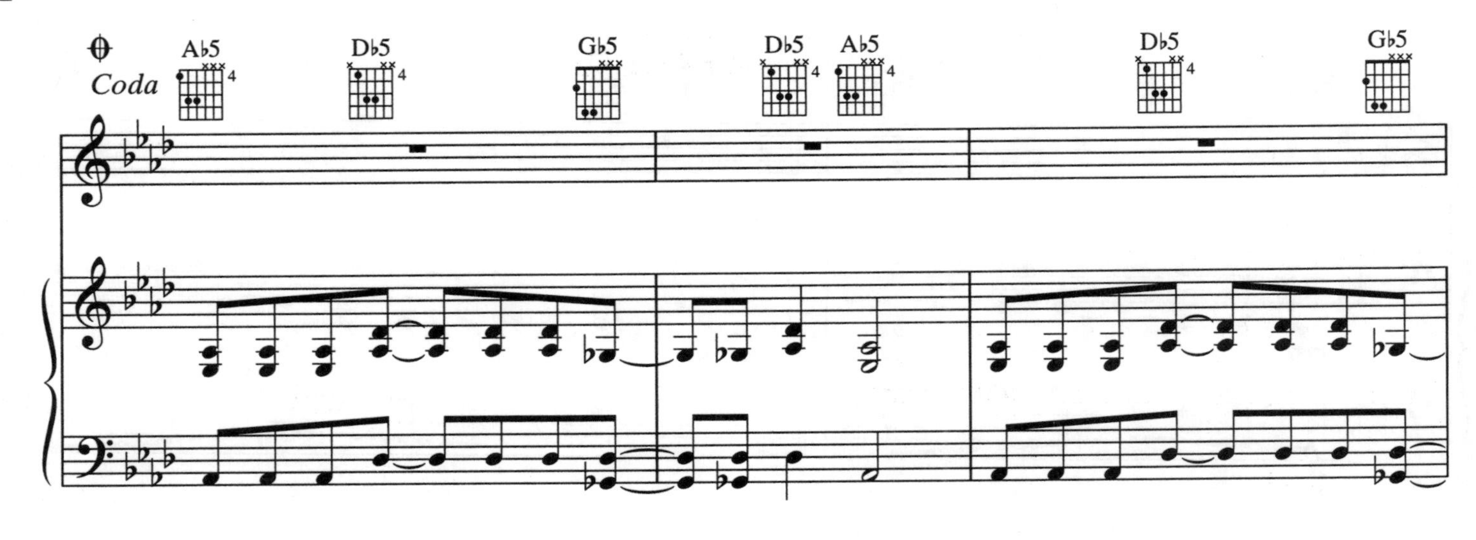

Coda
Ab5
Db5
Gb5
Db5
Ab5
Db5
Gb5

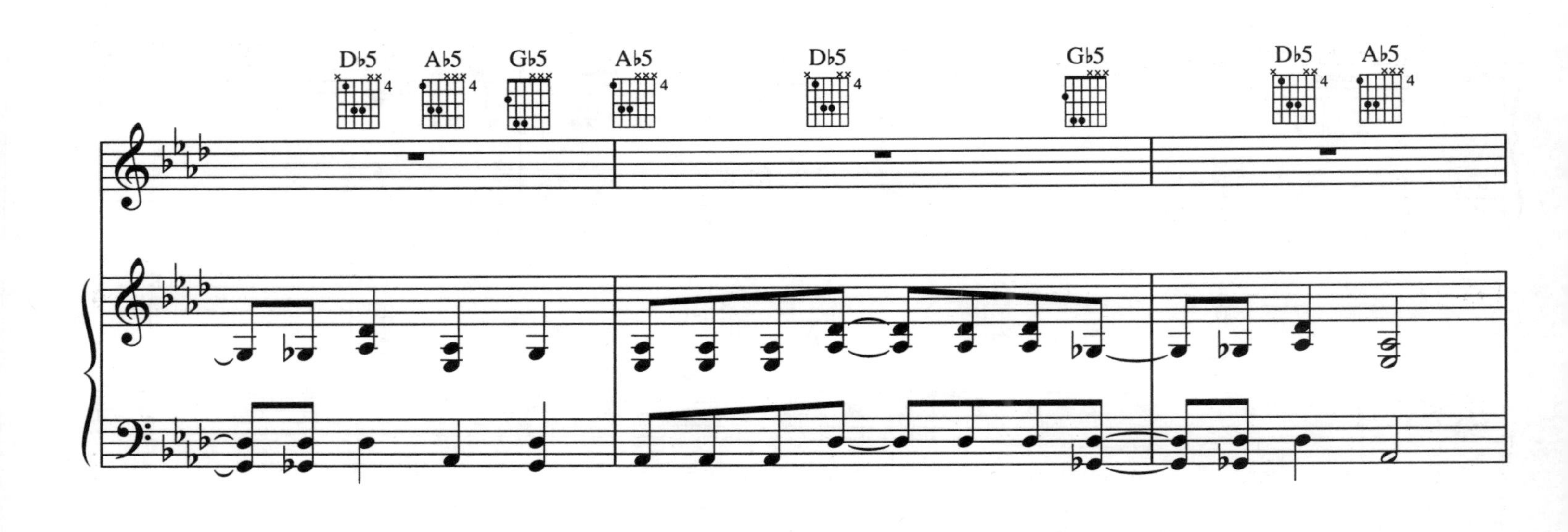

Db5
Ab5
Gb5
Ab5
Db5
Gb5
Db5
Ab5

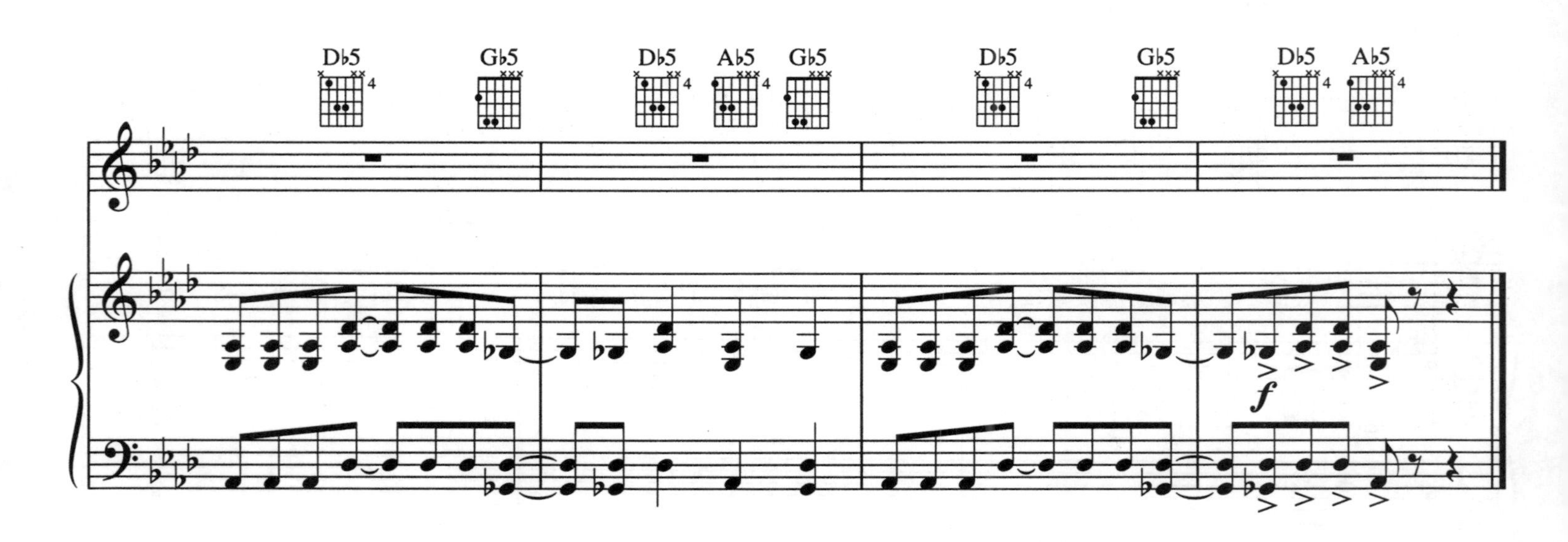

Db5
Gb5
Db5
Ab5
Gb5
Db5
Gb5
Db5
Ab5
f

ANIMALS

Gtr. in Drop D:
⑥ = D ③ = G
⑤ = A ② = B
④ = D ① = E

Lyrics by CHAD KROEGER
Music by NICKELBACK

Animals - 5 - 1

veins this train is com-ing off the track. I'll ask po - lite if the dev - il needs a
go by just how hard you wan-na squeeze. It's hard to steer when you're breath-ing in my
D5
ride be-cause the an - gel on my right ain't hang-ing out with me to - night. I'm driv-ing past your
ear but I got both hands on the wheel while you got both hands on my gear. By now, no
G5
C5
house while you were sneak-ing out, I got the car door o-pened up so you can jump in on the
doubt, that we were head-ing south. I guess no-bod-y ev - er taught her not to speak with a full
D5
G5
run. Your mom don't know that you were miss-ing, she'd be pissed if she could see the parts of
mouth, 'cause this was it, like flick-ing on a switch, it felt so good I al-most

Chorus:
C5 D5 F5 C5 G5 Bb5 C5 D5
you that I've been kiss - ing. Scream-in'
drove in - to the ditch. I'm scream-in'
no, we're nev - er gon - na quit, ain't noth - ing wrong with
F5 C5 G5 Bb5 C5 D5 F5 C5 G5
it. Just act - ing like we're an - i - mals.
No, no mat - ter where we
To Coda
Bb5 C5 D5 F5 C5 G5 Bb5 C5 D5
go, 'cause ev - 'ry - bod - y knows we're just a cou - ple an - i - mals.
F5 C5 G5 D5 F5 C5 G5
So, come on, ba - by, get in.

D5 F5 C5 G5
Get in, just get in.
Check out the trou-ble we're in.
Look at the trou-ble we're in.
D5 F5 C5 G5
1.
2.
D.S. 𝄋 al Coda
𝄌 Coda
D5 F5 C5 G5 B♭5 C5 D5
So, come on, ba-by, get in.
F5 C5 G5 B♭5 C5 D5 F5 C5 G5
Get in, just get in.
We're just a cou-ple an-i-mals.
Ain't noth-ing wrong with

Verse 3:
We were parked out by the tracks,
We're sitting in the back
And we just started getting busy
When she whispered, "What was that?"
The wind, I think, 'cause no one else knows where we are.
And that was when she started screamin',
"That's my dad outside the car!"
Oh, please, the keys, they're not in the ignition.
Must have wound up on the floor
While we were switching our positions.
I guess they knew that she was missing,
As I tried to tell her dad it was her mouth that I was kissing, screamin'...
(To Chorus:)

BEST I EVER HAD
(GREY SKY MORNING)

Gtr. tuned down 1/2 step:
⑥ = E♭ ③ = G♭
⑤ = A♭ ② = B♭
④ = D♭ ① = E♭

Words and Music by
MATTHEW SCANNELL

Am7 C(9) G D/F♯
G♯m7 B(9) F♯ C♯/E♯
in - to a grey sky morn - ing.
Now, I'm just a pho - ny. Re -
G Am7 C(9)
F♯ G♯m7 B(9)
Now, I'm here to stay. Love can be so bor -
mem - ber - ing the girl leaves me down and lone -
G D/F♯ Am Em7
F♯ C♯/E♯ G♯m D♯m7
ing. Noth - ing's quite the same now.
ly. Send it in a let - ter.
3. What was it you want - ed?
Chorus:
Am Em7 G
G♯m D♯m7 F♯
I just say your name now.
Make your - self feel bet - ter.
Could it be I'm haunt - ed?
But it's not so bad.

Am7
G♯m7
C(9)
B(9)
G
F♯
D/F♯
C♯/E♯
You're on - ly the best I ev - er had.
To Coda
You don't want me back.
(2.) You don't need me back.
(3.) I don't want you back.
You're just the best
1.
I ev - er had.
2.
Bridge:
F
E
I ev - er had.
And it may take

G
F♯
C
B
G/B
F♯/A♯
Am7
G♯m7
some time to patch me up in - side.
F
E
G
F♯
Dm
D♯m
But I can't take it so I run a - way and hide.
F
E
G
F♯
And I may find in time that you
D.S. 𝄋 al Coda
C
B
G/B
F♯/A♯
Am7
G♯m7
G
F♯
F
E
G
F♯
were al - ways right; you're al - ways right.

Coda
G
F♯
D/F♯
C♯/E♯
G
F♯
Am7
G♯m7
I ever had.
C(9)
B(9)
G
F♯
D/F♯
C♯/E♯
G
F♯
The best I ever had.
Am7
G♯m7
C(9)
B(9)
G
F♯
D/F♯
C♯/E♯
G
F♯
The best I ever...

BROKEN

Words and Music by
SHAUN WELGEMOED
and DALE STEWART

*Recorded in E♭ minor

Em
C(9)
I keep your pho - to - graph
and I know it serves me well.
There's so much left to learn
and no one left to fight.
D
I wan - na hold you high and steal your pain. Be - cause I'm
I wan - na hold you high and steal your pain. 'Cause I'm
Chorus:
C
(1.) bro - ken when I'm lone - some and I don't
(2.3.) bro - ken when I'm o - pen and I don't
feel right when you're gone a - way.
feel like I am
1.

C(9)
Em
C(9)
You've gone a - way.
You don't feel me
Em
C(9)
D
here
an - y - more.
2. 3.
C
Em
D
C
Em
D
strong e - nough.
'Cause I'm bro - ken
when I'm
C
Em
D
C
Em
D
To Coda
lone - some
and I don't feel right
when you're

C
Em
Cmaj9
Em
Cmaj9
gone a - way.
Em
Cmaj9
D
Em
Cmaj9
Em
Cmaj9
Em
Cmaj9
D
D.S.𝄋 al Coda
'Cause I'm
Coda
C
Em
C
Em
D
gone a - way.

C Em D C Em D C Em
'Cause I'm
C Em D C Em D C Em D
bro - ken when I'm lone - some and I don't feel right when you're
C Em Cmaj9 Em Cmaj9
gone. You've gone a - way. You don't feel me
gone a - way.
Em Cmaj9 D Em
here an - y - more.

BOULEVARD OF BROKEN DREAMS

Words by BILLIE JOE
Music by GREEN DAY

Fm
A♭
E♭
B♭
Don't know where it goes, but it's home to me and I walk a - lone.
mind. On the bor - der - line of the edge and where I walk a - lone.
Fm
A♭
E♭
B♭
Fm
A♭
E♭
B♭
I walk this emp - ty street on the bou - le - vard of bro - ken dreams,
Read be - tween the lines of what's f***ed up and ev - ery - thing's al -
Fm
A♭
E♭
B♭
where the cit - y sleeps and I'm the on - ly one and I walk a - lone.
right. Check my vi - tal signs and know I'm still a - live and I walk a - lone.

Fm
A♭
E♭
B♭
Fm
A♭
I walk a - lone, I walk a - lone.
Chorus:
E♭
B♭
A♭/C
D♭
A♭
I walk a - lone, I walk a...
My shad - ow's the on -
E♭
Fm
D♭
A♭
ly one that walks be - side me.
My shal - low heart's
E♭
Fm
D♭
A♭
the on - ly thing that's beat - ing.
Some - times I wish

To Coda
Eb
Fm
Db
Ab
some - one out there will find me.
'Til then I walk
C
N.C.
Fm
Ab
Eb
Bb
a - lone.
Ah. Ah. Ah. Ah.
1.
2.
Ab/C
Ah. Ah. Ah.
I walk a - lone, I walk a...
(Gtr. solo...

Eb
Fm
Db
Ab
Eb
Fm
Db
Ab
C
N.C.
...end solo)
Verse 3:
Fm
Ab
Eb
Bb
3. I walk this emp - ty street on the bou - le - vard of bro - ken dreams,

D.S. al Coda
Fm
Ab
Eb
Bb
Ab/C
where the cit - y sleeps and I'm the on - ly one and I walk a...
Coda
C
a - lone.
F5
Db
Eb2
Bb/D
f
1.2.3.
Ab5
E5
4.
Ab5
E5

DEVILS & DUST

Tune gtr. in Double Drop D:
⑥ = D ③ = G
⑤ = A ② = B
④ = D ① = D

Words and Music by
BRUCE SPRINGSTEEN

1.3.
A7sus
D(4)
Dsus
D(4)
Dsus
there's just dev-ils and dust.
dev-ils and dust.
2. We're a long, long way from
2.4.
Chorus:
D(4)
G
I've got God on my
We've got God on our
side,
and I'm / we're just try-ing to sur-
mf
D/F#
G
vive.
What if what you do to sur-vive kills the things you
A7sus
G
love? Fear's a pow-er-ful thing, it can turn your heart black, you can trust.

D/F♯
G
It - 'll take your God - filled soul,
A7sus
1.
D(4)
Dsus
D(4)
Dsus
fill it with dev-ils and dust.
D(4)
Dsus
D(4)
D.S. 𝄋
Dsus
2.
D(4)
Dsus
3. Well, I dreamed of you last dust.
D/F♯
G
A7sus
It - 'll take your God - filled soul,
fill it with dev-ils and

D(4)
Dsus
D(4)
Dsus
D(4)
Dsus
dust.
(Harmonica solo ad lib....
D(4)
Dsus
G
D(4)
Dsus
A7
D(4)
Dsus
1.
2.
Verses 5 & 6:
D(4)
Dsus
D(4)
Dsus
D(4)
Dsus
5. Now ev - 'ry wom-an and ev - 'ry man,
...end solo)
ger,

D(4)
G/D
they wan-na take a right-eous stand,
and to-night, faith just ain't e-nough.
find the love that God wills
When I look in-side my
D(4)
Dsus
A7
D(4)
Dsus
heart,
and the faith that he com-mands.
there's just dev-ils and dust.
1.
2.
Chorus:
D(4)
Dsus
D(4)
Dsus
G
6. I've got my fin-ger on the trig-
Well, I've got God on my side,
D/F♯
and I'm just try-ing to sur-vive.
What if what you do to sur-

G
A7
G
vive___ kills___ the things you love? Fear's__ a dan - ger-ous thing,__ it - 'll
D/F#
turn your heart_ black, you can trust.___ It - 'll take___ your God - filled_
G
A7
D(4)
Dsus
___ soul, fill it with dev-ils and_______ dust.__
D/F#
G
A7
It - 'll take__ your God - filled___ soul, fill it with dev-ils and____

Verse 3:
Well, I dreamed of you last night
In a field of blood and stone.
The blood began to dry,
And the smell began to rise.

Verse 4:
Well, I dreamed of you last night, Bob,
In a field of mud and bone.
Your blood began to dry
And the smell began to rise.
(To Chorus:)

All gtrs. in Drop D tuning:
⑥ = D ③ = G
⑤ = A ② = B
④ = D ① = E

DISAPPEAR

Words and Music by
DANIEL ESTRIN and
DOUGLAS ROBB

Moderately slow ♩ = 72

D Fmaj7 C5

mf

Fmaj7 C5 D5

Verses 1 & 2:

D Fmaj7 C5

1. There's a pain that sleeps in - side, it sleeps with just one eye
2. So I stand and look a - round, dis - tract - ed by the sounds

Fmaj7 C5 D5

and a - wak - ens the mo - ment that you leave.
of ev - 'ry - one, and ev - 'ry - thing I see.

Fmaj7
C5
Though I try to look a - way,
the pain, it still re - mains,
And I search through ev - 'ry face,
with - out a sin - gle trace
Fmaj7
C5
D5
on - ly leav - ing when you're next to me.
of the per - son, the per - son that I need.
Chorus:
D
C
G5
Do you know that ev - 'ry time you're near,
B♭5
G5
D
Dsus
D
ev - 'ry - bod - y else seems far a - way?

C
G5
So, can you come and make them dis-ap-pear?
B♭5
G5
1.
D
Dsus
D
Make them dis-ap-pear and we can stay.
2.
D
Dsus
D
Bridge:
B♭5
stay.
Can you make them dis-ap-pear,
C5
G5
make them dis-ap-pear?

F5
C5
Eb5
C5
G5
Woah, woah, woah.
F5
C5
Woah, woah,
Eb5
C5
G5
woah.
Verse 3:
D2
Fmaj7
C
3. There's a pain that sleeps in - side, it sleeps with just one eye
mf

Fmaj7
C
D2
D
and a - wak - ens the mo - ment that you leave.
D2
Fmaj7
C
And I search through ev - 'ry face, with - out a sin - gle trace
mp
Fmaj7
C
D5
of the per - son, the per - son that I need.
Chorus:
G5
5
F5
3
C5
10
Do you know that ev - 'ry time you're near,
f

Eb5
C5
10
G5
5
ev - 'ry - bod - y else seems far a - way?
F5
3
C5
10
So, can you come and make them dis - ap - pear?
Eb5
C5
10
G5
5
Make them dis - ap - pear and we can stay.
F5
3
C5
10
Woah, woah,

1.2.3.
E♭5
C5
10
G5
5
woah.
4.
G5
5
F5
3
C5
10
(Woah,
woah.)
Woah,
woah,
E♭5
C5
10
G5
5
Repeat ad lib. and fade
woah.

EVERYDAY

Words and Music by
JON BON JOVI, RICHIE SAMBORA
and ANDREAS CARLSSON

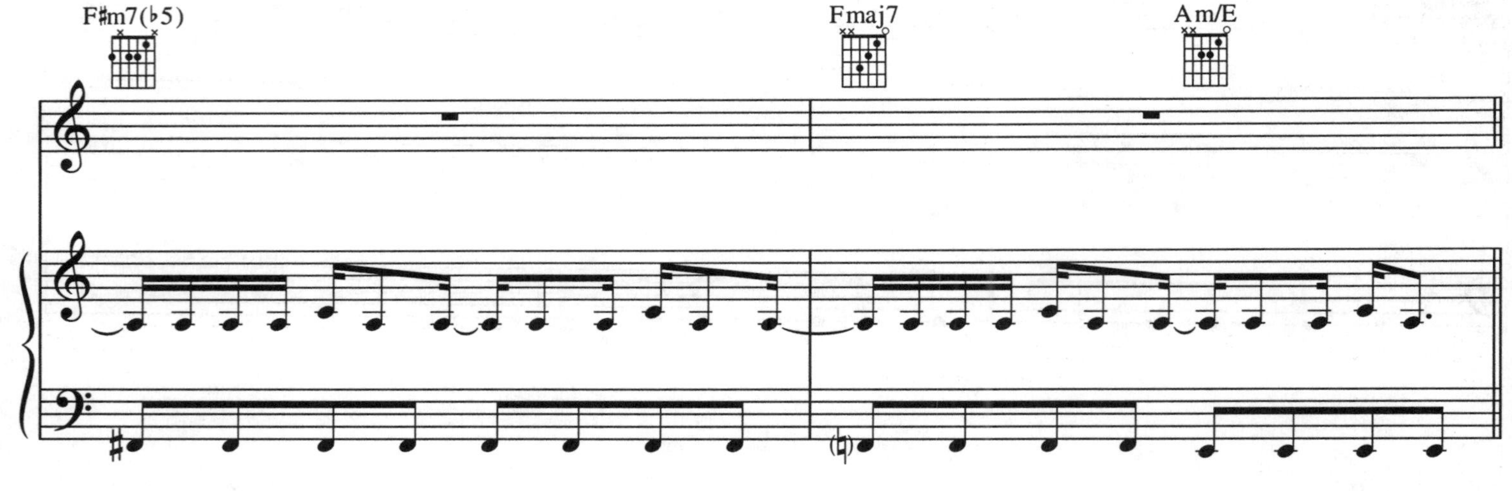

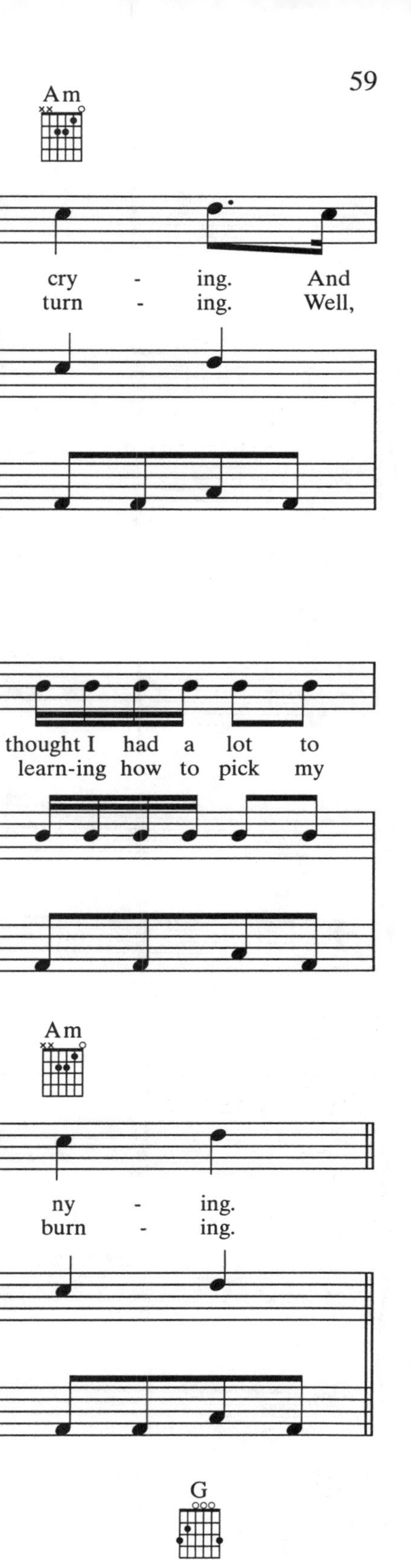
Am6
F/A
Am
side. I'd smile when I was cry - ing. And
same. Makes you won - der how the world keeps turn - ing. Well,
Am7
I had noth - ing but a lot to lose, thought I had a lot to
I'm learn - ing how to live my life, learn - ing how to pick my
Am6
F/A
Am
prove, in my life, there's no de - ny - ing.
fights, take my shots while I'm still burn - ing.

F
G
Good - bye to all my yes - ter - days.
Good - bye to all those rain - y nights.

F
Esus
Good - bye, so long, I'm on my way.
Good - bye, so long, I'm mov - in' on.
Chorus:
Am
C6
I had e - nough of cry - ing, bleed - ing, sweat - ing, dy - ing.
G2
F
Esus
Hear me when I say, gon - na live my life ev - 'ry day.
Am
C6
I'm gon - na touch the sky and I'll spread these wings and fly.

G2
1.
F
G2
I ain't here to play, gon - na live my life ev - 'ry day.
A5
2.
F
G2
live my life ev - 'ry day.
Hit the
Bridge:
Dm9
gas, take the wheel, I just made my - self a deal. There ain't
Fmaj7
N.C.
noth - ing gon - na get in my way. Ev - 'ry day.

Am
Am/G
(Guitar solo)
F♯m7(♭5)
1.
Fmaj7
Esus
2.
Fmaj7
Esus
F
Good - bye, so long,
Chorus:
Esus
Am
I'm mov - in' on. I had e - nough of cry - ing,

C6
G2
bleed - ing, sweat - ing, dy - ing.
Hear me when I say, gon - na
F
Esus
Am
live my life ev - 'ry day.
I'm gon - na touch the sky and
C6
G2
I'll spread these wings and fly.
I ain't here to play, gon - na
1.
F
G2
live my life ev - 'ry day.
2.
F
N.C.
live my life ev - 'ry day.

EVERYTHING YOU WANT

Words and Music by
MATT SCANNELL

Tune Guitar down one half step

G/B
C(9)
Am7
Em7
Gb/Bb
Cb(9)
Abm7
Ebm7
back of your mind. You nev-er could get it, un-less you were fed it.
1.
2.3.4.
Now you're here and you don't know why.
won't re - turn.
wish he'd say.
won't re - turn.
He's
Chorus:
Dsus
G
Gb
Dbsus
ev - 'ry - thing you want, he's ev - 'ry - thing you need. He's ev - 'ry - thing in - side of you that
you wish you could be. He says all the right things at ex - act - ly the right time. But

To Coda
1.
Am7 Em7 Dsus C(9) Am7 Em7
A♭m7 E♭m7 D♭sus C♭(9) A♭m7 E♭m7
he means noth - ing to you and you don't know why.
G/B C(9) Am7 Em7 G/B C(9)
G♭/B♭ C♭(9) A♭m7 E♭m7 G♭/B♭ C♭(9)
D.S.
2.
Dsus C(9)
D♭sus C♭(9)
don't know why.
Bridge:
Em7 C(9) Em7
E♭m7 C♭(9) E♭m7
But you'll just sit tight and watch it un - wind. It's on - ly what you're
D C(9) Em7 C(9)
D♭ C♭(9) E♭m7 C♭(9)
ask - ing for. And you'll be just fine with all of your time.

D.S.𝄋 al Coda
Em7
Ebm7
D
Db
C(9)
Cb(9)
It's on - ly what you're wait - ing for.
Coda
Dsus
Dbsus
Am7
Abm7
G
Gb
don't know why. I am ev - 'ry-thing you want. I am ev - 'ry-thing you need. I am
ev - 'ry-thing in - side of you that you wish you could be. I say all the right things at ex -
act - ly the right time. But I mean noth-ing to you and I don't know why.

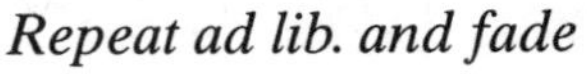

Verse 2:
But under skinned knees and the skid marks,
Past the places where you used to learn,
You howl and listen,
Listen and wait for the
Echoes of angels who won't return.
(To Chorus:)

Verse 3:
You're waiting for someone
To put you together.
You're waiting for someone
To push you away.
There's always another wound to discover.
There's always something more you'd wish he'd say.
(To Chorus:)

Verse 4:
Out of the island,
Into the highway,
Past the places where you might have turned.
You never did notice,
But you still hide away
The anger of angels who won't return.
(To Chorus:)

FOR YOU

Lyrics by
AARON LEWIS

Music by
AARON LEWIS, MICHAEL MUSHOK,
JONATHAN WYSOCKI and JOHN APRIL

E5 F#5 E5 F#5 E5 F#5
Eb5 F5 Eb5 F5 Eb5 F5
or it's your daugh - ter. Are my screams
one here to help me. But you don't
loud e - nough for you to hear
know how to lis - ten and let me
me? Should I turn this up for you?
make my de - ci - sions.
Chorus:
Dmaj7 A E
Dbmaj7 Ab Eb
I sit here locked in - side my head,

F#5
Dmaj7
A
E
F5
D♭maj7
A♭
E♭
re - mem - b'ring ev - 'ry - thing you've said.
This si - lence gets us no - where, gets
To Coda
1.
us no - where way too fast. 2. The si -
2.
Bridge:
N.C.
too fast.

All your in - sults and your curs - es make me feel
like I'm not a per - son. And I feel like I am noth -
ing. But you made me, so do some - thing. 'Cause I'm f***ed
F#5 E5 F#5 E5 F#5 E5 F#5 E5 F#5
F5 E♭5 F5 E♭5 F5 E♭5 F5 E♭5 F5
up be - cause you are, need at - ten -

E5
F#5
Eb5
F5
D.S. 𝄋 al Coda
tion,
at - ten - tion
you
could - n't
give.
Coda
A
Ab
E
Eb
too
fast.
G5
Gb5

FALLS APART

Words and Music by
SUGAR RAY and DAVID KAHNE

Verses 1 & 2:
F5 E5
B♭2 A2
F5 E5
1. She falls a - part by her - self; no one's there to
2. See additional lyrics
Dm7 C♯m7
Csus Bsus
F5 E5
B♭2 A2
talk or un - der - stand. Feels the sting, dries her eyes,
F5 E5
Dm7 C♯m7
Csus Bsus
Dm7 C♯m7
finds her - self, o - pens the door in - side. Peo - ple see
Csus Bsus
Dm7 C♯m7
Csus Bsus
right through you. Ev - 'ry - one who knew you well

F5
E5
Bb2
A2
F5
E5
falls apart, might as well, day is long and
Dm7
C#m7
Csus
Bsus
F5
E5
Bb2
A2
Chorus:
nothing is wasted. Run-a-way, run-a-way. (Run-a-way, run-a-way.)
F5
E5
Dm7
C#m7
Csus
Bsus
F5
E5
Hold on to you, but you're going away. Run-a-way, run-a-way.
Bb2
A2
F5
E5
To Coda
1.
Dm7
C#m7
Csus
Bsus
F5
E5
(Run-a-way, run-a-way.) Hold you to-mor-row, but you're leav-ing to-day.

2.
Bridge:
Dm7
Csus
A
B♭
C♯m7
Bsus
G♯
A
leav-ing to-day.
Some-times we feel a-round, it's get-ting I can't be down.
C
B
All this time I'd be on my own.
An-y thought of be-ing, yeah, it's
time a-way, so I'd a-fraid I no-where to, no-where to, no-where to, no-where,
F5
E5
N.C.
yeah.

Verse 3:
F5
E5
B♭2
A2
F5
E5
3. She falls a - part, no one's there, hold her hand, it
Dm7
C♯m7
Csus
Bsus
Am
G♯m
Dm7
C♯m7
seems to dis - ap - pear. Falls a - part, might as well,
Am
G♯m
Dm7
C♯m7
N.C.
D.S. 𝄋 al Coda
day is long and noth - ing is wast - ed.

Verse 2:
You walk along by yourself.
There's no sound, nothing's changing.
They've gone away, left you there.
Emptiness, there's nothing you can share.
All those words that hurt you
More than you would let it show.
It comes apart by itself.
Always will and everything's wasted.
(To Chorus:)

FEELIN' WAY TOO DAMN GOOD

Gtrs. in Drop D tuning:

⑥ = D ③ = G
⑤ = A ② = B
④ = D ① = E

Lyrics by CHAD KROEGER
Music by NICKELBACK

B♭
C
G5
now that you're here, I just feel like I'm con - stant - ly dream - ing.
got - ta make love just one last time in the show - er.
Well, some-thing's
F5
G5
1.
D
got - ta go wrong 'cause I'm feel - in' way too damn good.
2. For
2.3.4.
D5
Chorus:
B♭5
F5
And it's like ev - 'ry time I turn a - round
C5
G5
F5
G5
I fall in love and find my heart face down and where it lands is where it should.

F5
D5
F5
D5
B♭5
F5
Oo.
This time it's like
C5
G5
the two of us should prob - 'bly start to fight 'cause some - thing's
F5
G5
To Coda
got - ta go wrong 'cause I'm feel - in' way too damn good.
D
D/C
G/B
Gm/B♭
Oh!
Feel - in' way too damn good.

D
D/C
1.
G/B
Gm/B♭
D.S. 𝄋
2.
G/B
Gm/B♭
D
D/C
Do, do, do, do, do, do,
do, do, do, do, do, do.
G/B
Gm/B♭
D
D/C
Do, do, do, do, do, do,
do, do, do,
do, do, do.
Do, do, do, do, do, do,
do, do, do, do, do, do.
G/B
Gm/B♭
D.C. al Coda
Do, do, do,
do, do, do,
do, do, do,
do, do,
do,

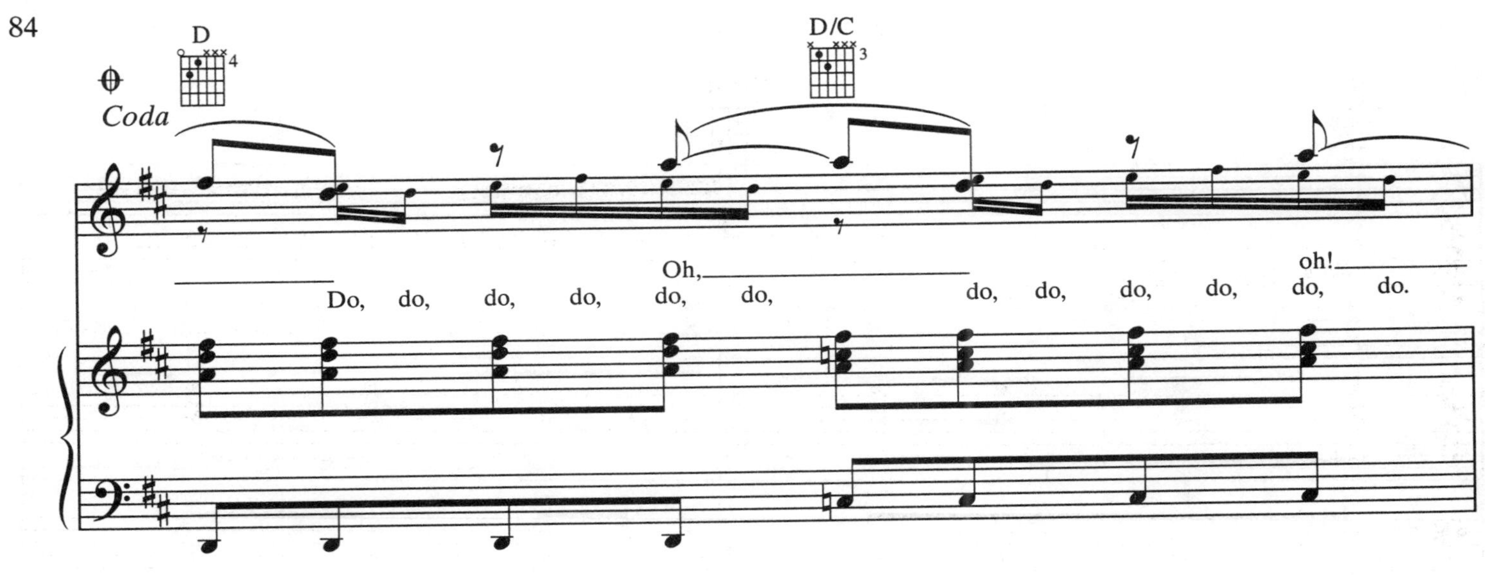
D
D/C
Coda
Oh,
oh!
Do, do, do, do, do, do,
do, do, do, do, do, do.

G/B
Gm/B♭
I'm feel - in' way too damn good!
Do, do, do, do, do, do, do, do, do,
do, do, do. I

D
D/C
missed you so much that I begged you to fly and see

Verse 3:
Sometimes I think best if left in the memory.
It's better kept inside than left for good.
Looking back each time they tried to tell me.
Well, something's gotta go wrong,
'Cause I'm feelin' way too damn good.
(To Chorus:)

From the Columbia Pictures Motion Picture SPIDER-MAN

HERO

Words and Music by
CHAD KROEGER

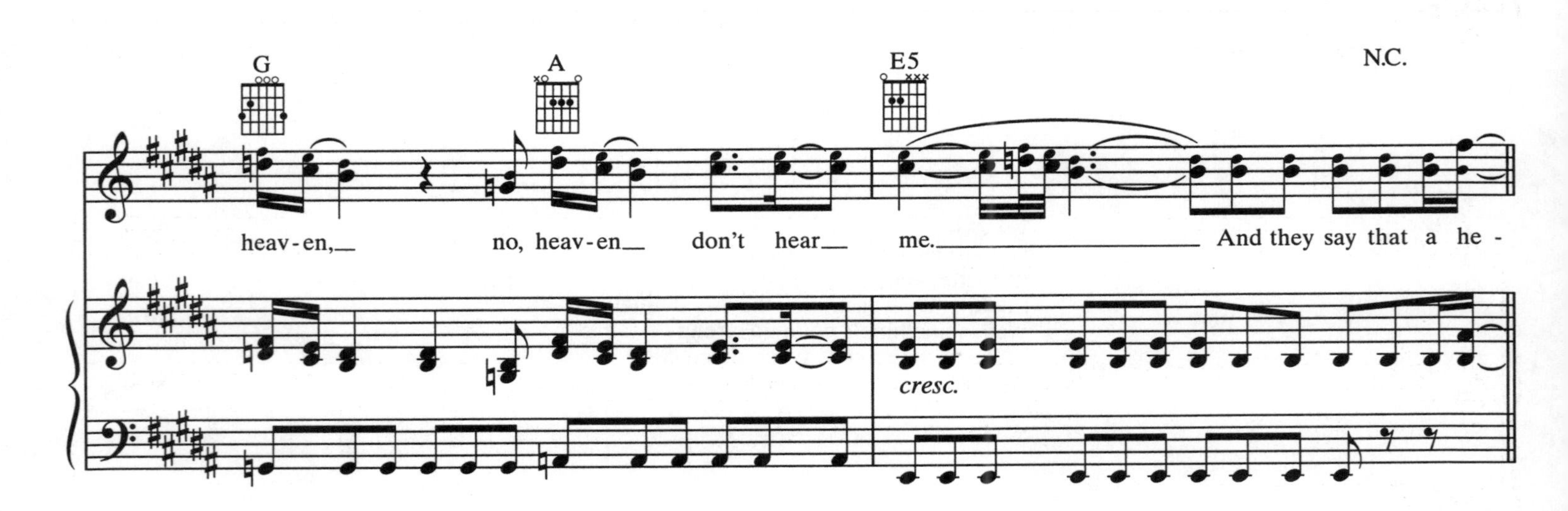

Chorus:
G
A
B
A
ro could save_ us. I'm not gon-na stand_ here and wait.___ I'll hold on to the wings_
f
G
A
E5
N.C.
___ of the ea - gles. Watch as we all_ fly a - way.___
Verse 2:
G♯m
E
Some-one told_ me_ love would all save us.___
mf
G♯m
E
But how can that_ be? Look what love_ gave us.___ A world full of

G
A
E5
N.C.
kill - ing and blood spill - ing; that world nev - er came. And they say that a he -
cresc.
Chorus:
G
A
B
A
ro could save us. I'm not gon-na stand here and wait. I'll hold on to the wings
f
G
A
E5
of the ea - gles. Watch as we all fly a - way. Ah,
Solo:
G
A
B
A
ah.
(Inst. solo ad lib....

G
A
E5
N.C.
...end solo) Now that the world
mp
Bridge:
G
A
B
isn't ending, it's love that I'm sending to you.
It isn't the love
G
A
E5
N.C.
of a hero, and that's why I fear it won't do.
And they say that a he-
cresc.
Chorus:
G
A
ro could save us. I'm not gonna stand here and wait.
f

B
A
I'll hold on to the wings
G
A
of the ea - gles. Watch as we all fly a - way.
E5
And they're watch - ing us.
G
A
They're watch - ing us as we all fly a - way.
Watch - ing us, they're all watch - ing us.

1.
B
And they're watch - ing us.
2.
B
And they're watch - ing us.
G
A
They're watch - ing us as we all fly a - way,
Watch - ing us, they're all watch - ing us.
E5
B
yeah, yeah, woah.
decresc.
rit.
mf

HOLIDAY

Words by BILLIE JOE
Music by GREEN DAY

Verse:
Fm Db5 Ab5 Eb Fm Db5
1. Hear the sound of the fall - ing rain com - ing down like an
2. Hear the drum pound-ing out of time, an - oth - er pro - test -
Ab5 C5 Fm Db5 Ab5 Eb
Ar - ma - ged - don flame. (Hey.) The shame, the ones who died with -
or has crossed the line (Hey.) to find the mon - ey's on the
C5 Fm Db5
out a name.
oth - er side.
Hear the dogs howl - ing
Can I get an -
Ab5 Eb Fm Db5 Ab5 C5
out of key to a hymn called "Faith and mis - er -
oth - er "A - men?" (A - men.) There's a flag wrapped a - round a score of

Fm
Db5
Ab5
Eb
C5
y," (Hey.) and bleed, the com - pa - ny lost the war to - day.
men. (Hey.) A gag, a plas - tic bag on a mon - u - ment.
Chorus:
F5
Db5
I beg to dream and dif - fer
Ab5
Eb5
F5
from the hol - low lies.
This is the dawn-
Db5
Ab5
C5
ing of the rest of our lives

1.
N.C.
Fm
D♭
A♭
E♭
on hol - i - day.
mf
Fm
D♭
A♭
E♭
2.
N.C.
on hol - i - day.
F5
A♭5
D♭5
B♭5
E♭5
C5
F5
A♭5
E♭5
C5
F5
Hey.
F5
A♭5
D♭5
B♭5
E♭5
C5
F5
A♭5
E♭5
C5
F5

D♭
A♭
C
(Guitar solo)
F5
E♭5
D♭
A♭
C
(Ooh.
)
N.C.
mp
3

The rep - re - sen - ta - tive from Cal - i - for - nia has the floor.
Bridge:
Zieg Heil to the Pres - i - dent gas - man, bombs a - way is your pun - ish - ment.
mf
Pul - ver - ize the Eif - fel Tow - ers, who crit - i - cize your gov - ern - ment.
Bang, bang goes the bro - ken glass and kill all the fags that don't a - gree.

Eb5
C5
F5
Bb5
Tri - als by fire___ set - ting fire___ is not a way that's meant for me.
C5
Bb5
C5
Just cause, just 'cause, be -
(Hey, hey, hey, hey, hey, hey,
Chorus:
F5
Db5
cause we're out - laws, yeah. I beg to dream and___ dif - fer___
hey, hey.)
f
Ab5
Eb5
F5
Db5
from the hol - low___ lies.___ This is the dawn___ ing___ of___ the___

*Sustained chord segues to "Boulevard Of Broken Dreams."

HOW YOU REMIND ME

Drop D tuning: ⑥ = D

Lyrics by CHAD KROEGER
Music by NICKELBACK

B♭5
E♭2
C5
F2
me of what I real-ly am. This is how you re-mind me of what I real-ly am.
Chorus:
E♭5
F5
It's not like you to say sor-ry. I was wait-ing on a dif-f'rent sto-ry.
This time I'm mis-tak-en for hand-ing you a heart worth break-ing.
And I've been wrong, I've been down, been to the bot-tom of ev-'ry bot-tle.

C5
Eb5
Bb5
F5
To Coda
These five words in my head scream, "Are we hav - in' fun yet?"
Yeah, yeah, yeah, no, no. Yeah, yeah,
1.
2.
yeah, no, no. yeah, no, no. Yeah, yeah,
yeah, no, no. Yeah, yeah, yeah, no, no.

C2
F2
B♭2
E♭2
C2
F2
B♭2
E♭2
C2
F2
1. Nev - er made it as a wise man,
B♭2
E♭2
C2
A♭2
I could-n't cut it as a poor man steal - in'. And this is how you re - mind
B♭2
C2
A♭2
B♭2
D.S. 𝄋 al Coda
me. This is how you re - mind me.

Verse 2:
It's not like you didn't know that.
I said I love you and swear I still do.
And it must have been so bad.
'Cause livin' with me must have damn near killed you.
This is how you remind me of what I really am.
This is how you remind me of what I really am.
(To Chorus:)

From the VH1 Original Movie AT ANY COST

PINCH ME

Words and Music by
STEVEN PAGE and ED ROBERTSON

F
G
C(9)
F/A
C/G
F
G
con-sid-'ring ev - 'ry - thing's a mess.
There's a res - t'rant down the
mf
C(9)
F
C/E
F
G
C(9)
F/A
C
street
where hun-gry peo - ple like to eat.
F
G
C(9)
F/A
C/G
I could walk, but I'll just drive;
D7/F♯
F
G
it's cold - er than it looks out - side.
cresc.

Chorus:
C
G
F
D
It's like a dream, you try to re-mem-ber, but it's gone, then you try to scream, but it on-ly comes out as a yawn, when you
tacet 1x
Pinch me.
Pinch me,
f
C
G
F
G
try to see the world be - yond your front door.
I'm still a - sleep.
C
G
F
D
To Coda
Take your time 'cause the way I rhyme's gon-na make you smile, when you re-al-ize that a guy my size might take a while, just to
Please, God, tell me

1.
C
G
F
F6/9
try to fig - ure out what all this is for.
dim.

2.
C
G
F
G
try to fig - ure out what all this is for.
Pinch me.
I'm still a - sleep.

Bridge:
Am
G
F
G
Am
G
Pinch me, 'cause I'm still a - sleep.

F
G
Am
G
Please, God, tell me
D.S. 𝄋 al Coda
that I'm still a - sleep.
Coda
C
Try to fig - ure out what all this is for.
I'm still a - sleep.

C
G
F
G
Try to fig - ure out what all this is for.
I'm still a - sleep.
C
G
F
G
Try to see the world be - yond your front door.
I'm still a - sleep.
C
G
D
Try to fig - ure out what all this is for.
I'm still a - sleep.

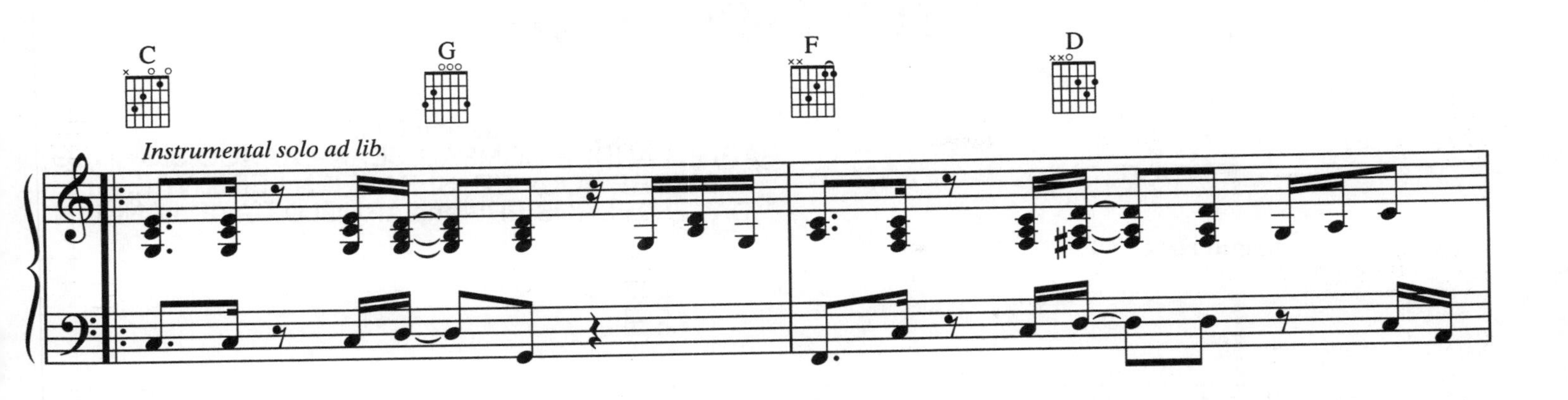

Verse 2:
It's the perfect time of day
To throw all your cares away;
Put the sprinkler on the lawn
And run through with my gym shorts on.
Take a drink right from the hose
And change into some dryer clothes;
Climb the stairs up to my room,
Sleep away the afternoon.
(To Chorus:)

Verse 3:
On an evening such as this,
It's hard to tell if I exist.
If I pack the car and leave this town,
Who'll notice that I'm not around?
I could hide out under there.
(I just made you say underwear.)
I could leave but I'll just stay,
All my stuff's here anyway.
(To Chorus:)

I'D DO ANYTHING

Gtr. tuned down 1/2 step:
⑥ = E♭ ③ = G♭
⑤ = A♭ ② = B♭
④ = D♭ ① = E♭

Words and Music by
CHARLES-ANDRE COMEAU, JEAN-FRANCOIS STINCO,
PIERRE BOUVIER, SEBASTIEN LEFEBVRE,
DAVID DESROSIERS and ARNOLD DAVID LANNI

Bright rock ♩ = 160

Guitar → A5, A5, A
Piano → N.C., A♭5, N.C., A♭5, N.C., A♭

mf

𝄋 *Verse:*

A/G♯ (A♭/G), F♯m7 (Fm7), D (D♭)

1. An - oth - er day___ is go - ing by.___ I'm think - ing a - bout_
2. To - geth - er we___ broke all the rules.___ Dream - ing of drop -

(Bass tacet first time)

E
A
A/G#
F#m7
E♭
A♭
A♭/G
Fm7
you all the time. But you're out there, and I'm here wait -
ping out of school, and leave this place, to nev - er come
D
E
A
A/G#
D♭
E♭
A♭
A♭/G
ing. And I wrote this let -
back. So now, may - be af -
(Bass play every time)
F#m7
D
E
A
Fm7
D♭
E♭
A♭
ter in my head, 'cause so man - y things were left un - said.
ter all these years, if you miss me, have no fear;
A/G#
F#m7
D
A♭/G
Fm7
D♭
But now you're gone, and I can't think straight.
I'll be here, I'll be wait - ing.

E
Bm7
A/C#
D
E
E♭
B♭m7
A♭/C
D♭
E♭
This could be the one last chance to make you un - der-stand,
1.
To Next Strain
2.
Esus
E5
Bm7
A/C#
E♭sus
E♭5
B♭m7
A♭/C
yeah.
and I just can't let you leave
D
E
Esus
E5
D♭
E♭
E♭sus
E♭5
me once a - gain,
yeah.
Chorus:
D5
A
E
F#m7
D♭5
N.C.
A♭
E♭
Fm7
I'd do an - y - thing just to hold

D A
D♭ A♭
you in my arms, to try to make you laugh.
E F♯m7 D
E♭ Fm7 D♭ N.C.
Some - how, I can't put you in the past. I'd do
A E F♯m7
A♭ E♭ Fm7
an - y - thing just to fall a - sleep with you.
D A E F♯m7
D♭ A♭ E♭ Fm7
Will you re - mem - ber me? 'Cause I know I won't

1.
D.S. 𝄋
2.
D
D♭
N.C.
A
A♭
D
D♭
for - get you.
Bridge:
D2
D♭2
A
A♭
E
E♭
F♯m7
Fm7
I close my eyes, and all I see is you.
I close my eyes; I try to sleep. I can't for - get you.
Na na na, na na na. And I'd do an - y - thing for you.

D2 A E
D♭2 A♭ E♭
Na na na, na na na na.
Chorus:
D5 E F♯m7
D♭5 N.C. E♭ Fm7
I'd do any-y-thing just to hold
D A
D♭ A♭
you in my arms, to try to make you laugh.
E F♯m7 D
E♭ Fm7 D♭
Some-how, I can't put you in the past. I'd do

A
E
F#m7
Ab
Eb
Fm7
anything just to fall asleep with you,
D
A
E
Db
Ab
Eb
to fall asleep with you, with you,
F#m7
D
A
E
Fm7
Db
Ab
Eb
oh yeah. I'd do anything
F#m7
D
A
Fm7
Db
Ab
to fall asleep with you. I'd do

E
F#m7
Eb
Fm7
an - y - thing.
There's noth - ing I won't
D
A
E
F#m7
Db
Ab
Eb
Fm7
do. I'd do an - y - thing
to fall a - sleep with
D
A
E
F#m7
Db
Ab
Eb
Fm7
you. I'd do an - y - thing,
'cause I know I won't
D
A5
Db
N.C.
Ab5
for - get you.

IT'S BEEN AWHILE

Words and Music by
AARON LEWIS, MICHAEL MUSHOK,
JONATHAN WYSOCKI and JOHN APRIL

Cmaj7
Bmaj7
Gmaj7
F♯maj7
Am7/D
G♯m7/C♯
since I could hold my head up high.
Asus
G♯sus
Cmaj7
Bmaj7
Gmaj7
F♯maj7
And it's been a while since I first saw you.
Am7/D
G♯m7/C♯
Asus
G♯sus
Cmaj7
Bmaj7
And it's been a while since I could stand
Gmaj7
F♯maj7
Am7/D
G♯m7/C♯
Asus
G♯sus
on my own two feet again. And it's been a while

Cmaj7
Bmaj7
Gmaj7
F#maj7
Am7/D
G#m7/C#
since I could call you.
Chorus:
Am
G#m
C
B
G
F#
1.2. And ev - 'ry - thing I can't re - mem - ber,
3. See additional lyrics for Last Chorus
D7
C#7
Am
G#m
C
B
as f***ed up as it all may seem,
G
F#
D7
C#7
Am
G#m
the con - se - quenc -

C
G
D7
B
F♯
C♯7
es that___ I've ren - dered,
Am
C
G
To Coda
G♯m
B
F♯
I stretched my - self___ be - yond___ my means.___
I've gone and f***ed___ things up___ a - gain.___
1. D7
2. D7
Bridge:
G
C♯7
C♯7
F♯
D7
Am
C♯7
G♯m
Why must I feel___ this way?_

G
F♯
D7
C♯7
Am
G♯m
Just
make this go a - way.
G
F♯
D7
C♯7
Am
G♯m
Just one more peace - ful day.
G
F♯
D7
C♯7
Am
G♯m
D.S. 𝄋 al Coda

Verse 2:
And it's been a while since I could say that I wasn't addicted.
And it's been a while since I could say I loved myself as well.
And it's been a while since I've gone and f***ed thing up just like I always do.
And it's been a while, but all that sh** seems to disappear when I'm with you.
(To Chorus:)

Verse 3:
And it's been a while since I could look at myself straight.
And it's been a while since I said I'm sorry.
And it's been a while since I've seen the way the candles light your face.
And it's been a while, but I can still remember just the way you taste.

Last Chorus:
And everything I can't remember,
As f***ed up as it all may seem to be, I know it's me.
I cannot blame this on my father.
He did the best he could for me.
(To Outro:)

All gtrs. in Drop D, down 1/2 step:

⑥ = D♭ ③ = G♭
⑤ = A♭ ② = B♭
④ = D♭ ① = E♭

ONE THING

Words and Music by
SCOTT ANDERSON
and JAMES BLACK

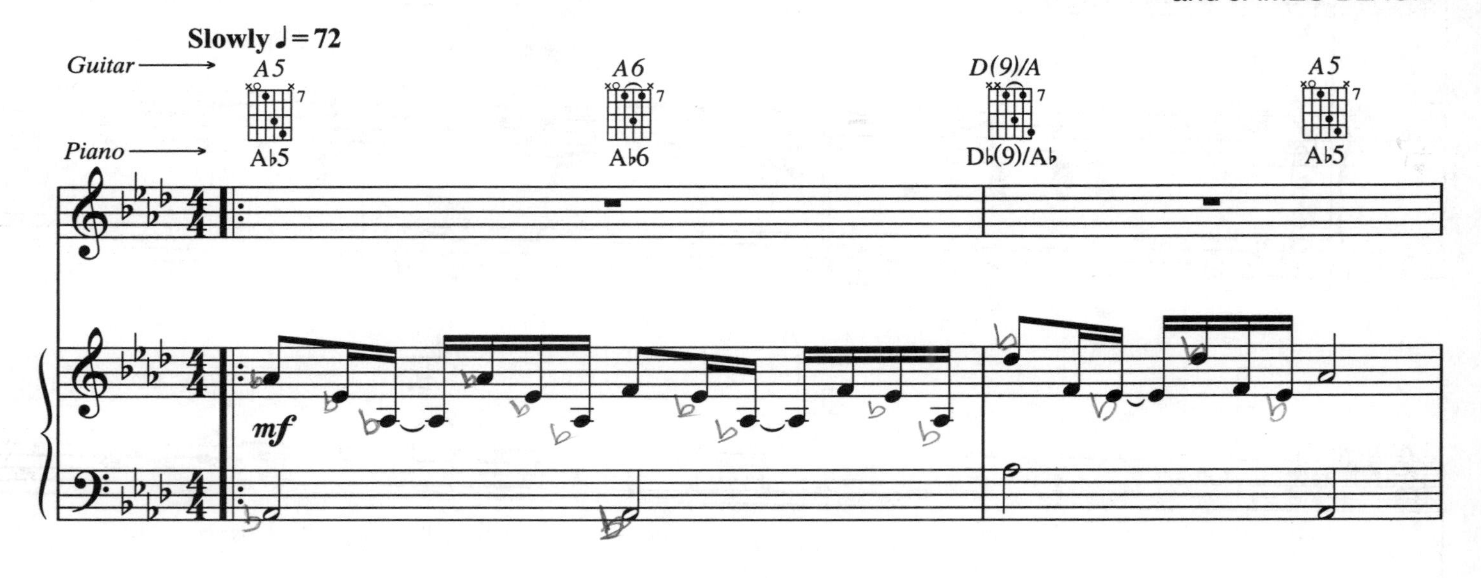

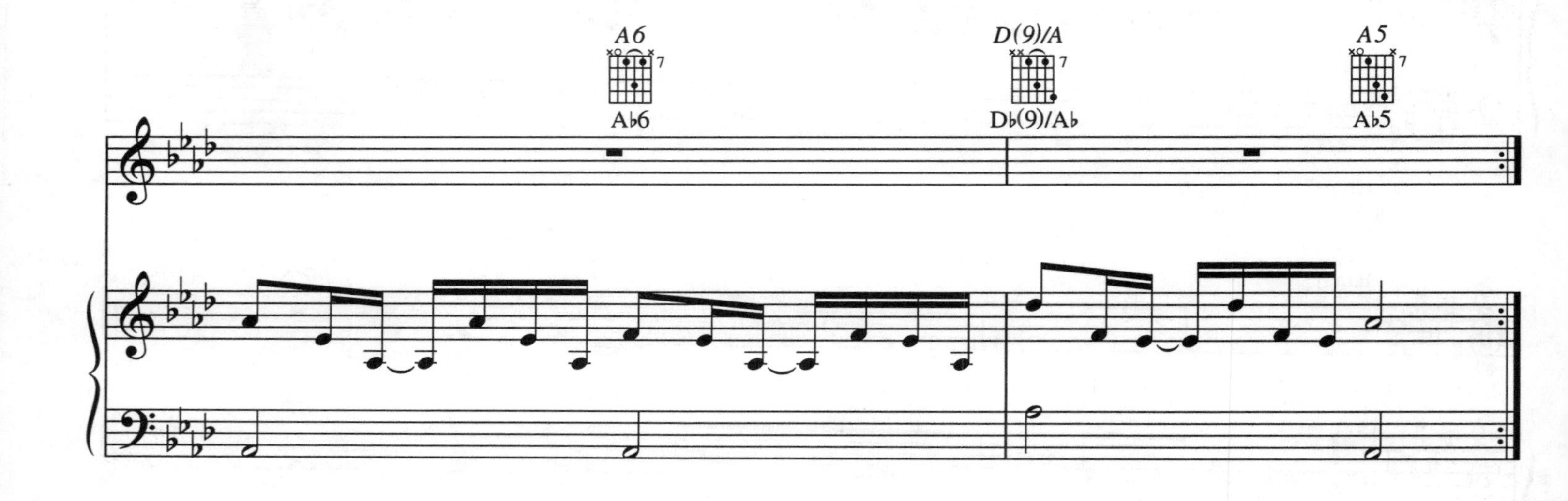

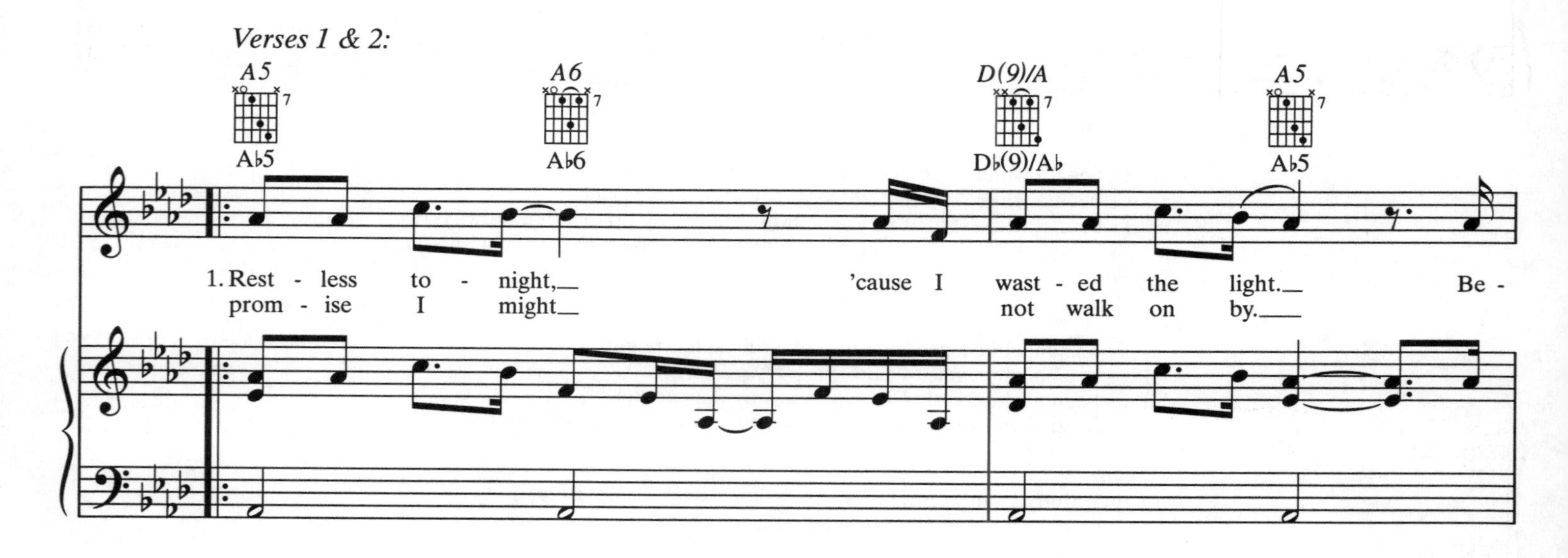

A6
A♭6
D(9)/A
D♭(9)/A♭
A5
A♭5
tween both these times, I drew a real - ly thin line. It's
May - be next time, but not this time.
noth - ing I planned, and not that I can. But
E - ven though I know, I don't wan - na know.
you should be mine a - cross that line.
Yeah, I guess I know, I just hate how it sounds.
If I
Chorus:
trad - ed it all, if I gave it all a - way for

D6/9/A
Db6/9/Ab
one thing, just for one thing. If I
A5
Ab5
sort - ed it out, if I knew all a - bout this
D6/9/A
Db6/9/Ab
1.
D6/9
Db6/9
one thing, would-n't that be some - thing. 2. I
2.
G
Gb
A5
Ab5
some - thing. If I trad - ed it all, if I

D6/9/A
Db6/9/Ab
gave it all a - way for one thing, just for
D6/9
Db6/9
A5
Ab5
one thing. If I sort - ed it out, if I
D6/9/A
Db6/9/Ab
knew all a - bout this one thing, would-n't that be
Verse 3:
D6/9
Db6/9
A5
Ab5
A6
Ab6
some - thing. 3. E - ven though I know,

D(9)/A
A5
A6
D♭(9)/A♭
A♭5
A♭6
I don't wan-na know.
Yeah, I guess I know, I just
hate how it sounds.
E - ven though I know,
I don't wan-na know.
Yeah, I guess I know, I just
hate how it sounds.
If I

Chorus:
A5
A♭5
trad - ed it all, if I gave it all a - way for
D6/9/A
D♭6/9/A♭
one thing, just for one thing. If I
A5
A♭5
sort - ed it out, if I knew all a - bout this
D6/9/A
D♭6/9/A♭
Repeat ad lib. and fade
D6/9
D♭6/9
one thing, would-n't that be some - thing. If I

Gtr. tuned down 1/2 step:
⑥ = E♭ ③ = G♭
⑤ = A♭ ② = B♭
④ = D♭ ① = E♭

PERFECT

Words and Music by
CHARLES-ANDRE COMEAU, JEAN-FRANCOIS STINCO,
PIERRE BOUVIER, SEBASTIEN LEFEBVRE,
DAVID DESROSIERS and ARNOLD DAVID LANNI

Verse:
E
Eb
A
Ab
1. Hey, Dad, look at me, think back, and talk to me. Did I
2. I try not to think a - bout the pain I feel in - side. Did you
grow up ac - cord - ing to plan? And do you
know you used to be my he - ro? All the
think I'm wast - ing my time do - ing things I wan - na do? But, it
days you spent with me now seem so far a - way, and it
hurts when you dis - ap - prove all a - long. And now
feels like you don't care an - y - more. And now

F#m7
E/G#
A
Fm7
E♭/G
A♭
I try hard to make it. I just wan - na make you
I try hard to make it. I just wan - na make you
E
E♭
proud. I'm nev - er gon - na be good e - nough for
proud. I'm nev - er gon - na be good e - nough for
F#m7
E/G#
A
Fm7
E♭/G
A♭
you. Can't pre-tend that I'm all right. And you can't change me.
you. I can't stand an - oth - er fight. And noth - in's all right.
'Cause we
Chorus:
E
B
C#m7
E♭
B♭
Cm7
lost it all. Noth-ing lasts for - ev - er. I'm sor - ry; I can't be

A(9)
A♭(9)
E
E♭
B
B♭
per - fect. Now it's just too late, and we can't go back. I'm sor -
1.
C#m7
Cm7
A(9)
A♭(9)
E
E♭
ry; I can't be per - fect.
A
A♭
E
E♭
A
A♭
2.
C#m7
Cm7
B
B♭
ry; I can't be per - fect.

Bridge:
A
B
E
A
B
E
A♭
B♭
E♭
A♭
B♭
E♭
Noth-ing's gon-na change the things__ that you said.
And noth-ing's gon-na make this right__
__ a - gain._
C#m7
Cm7
B
B♭
A
A♭
Please don't turn your back. I can't__ be-lieve it's hard just to talk_
__ to you, but you don't un-der - stand.
A(9)
A♭(9)
E
E♭
Emaj7
E♭maj7
E
E♭
A
A♭
Amaj7
A♭maj7
A
A♭
E
E♭
Emaj7
E♭maj7
E
E♭
A
A♭
Amaj7
A♭maj7
A
A♭
'Cause we

Chorus:
E
B
C#m7
E♭
B♭
Cm7
lost it___ all.___ Noth-ing lasts for - ev - er. I'm sor - ry; I can't___ be
A(9)
E
B
A♭(9)
E♭
B♭
per - fect. Now it's just too___ late,___ and we can't go___ back.___ I'm sor -
C#m7
1.
A(9)
2.
A(9)
Cm7
A♭(9)
A♭(9)
ry; I can't___ be per - fect. 'Cause we per - fect.

ABSOLUTELY
(Story of a Girl)

Words and Music by
JOHN HAMPSON

Verse:
G
D
C
Bm
C2
1. How man - y days_ in a year_ she
(2.) how man - y lov - ers would stay_ just to
3. (Inst. solo ad lib. . . .
G5
D
Bm
C2
woke up with hope_ and she on - ly found tears? And I can be so_ in - sin - cere,
put up with this_ sh** day_ af - ter day? How did we wind_ up this_ way,
G5
D
Bm
C2
mak - ing her prom - is - es nev - er for real,_ as long as she stays_ there wait - ing,
watch - ing our mouths_ for the words_ that we say?_ As long as we stand_ here wait - ing,
G5
D
Bm
C2
wear - ing the holes_ in the soles_ of her shoes._ How man - y days_ dis - ap - pear when you
wear - ing the clothes_ of the souls_ that we choose,_ how do we get_ there to - day, when we're

G5
D
Em7
D/F♯
look in the mir - ror, so how__ do you choose?__
walk-ing too far__ for the price__ of our shoes?__
. . . end solo)
Your clothes nev - er wear as well__ the next day and your
G
A7sus
Em7
D/F♯
hair nev-er falls in quite__the same way. But you nev - er seem__ to run__ out of things__ to say.__
A7sus
N.C.
Chorus:
C2
G5
__ This is the sto - ry of a girl who cried a riv - er and drowned__
A7sus
D
Bm
C2
To Coda
__ the whole world. And while she looks__ so sad__
1.3. in pho - to - graphs,__
2. and lone - ly there,__
I

1.
A7sus
G
D
C
ab - so - lute - ly love her when she smiles.
G
D
C
2.
Em7
D/F♯
2. Now, smiles.
G5
A7sus
Em7
D/F♯
A7sus
D.S. 𝄋 al Coda
N.C.

Coda
A7sus
N.C.
C2
G5
ab - so - lute - ly love her. This is the sto - ry of a girl, her pret - ty face she hid

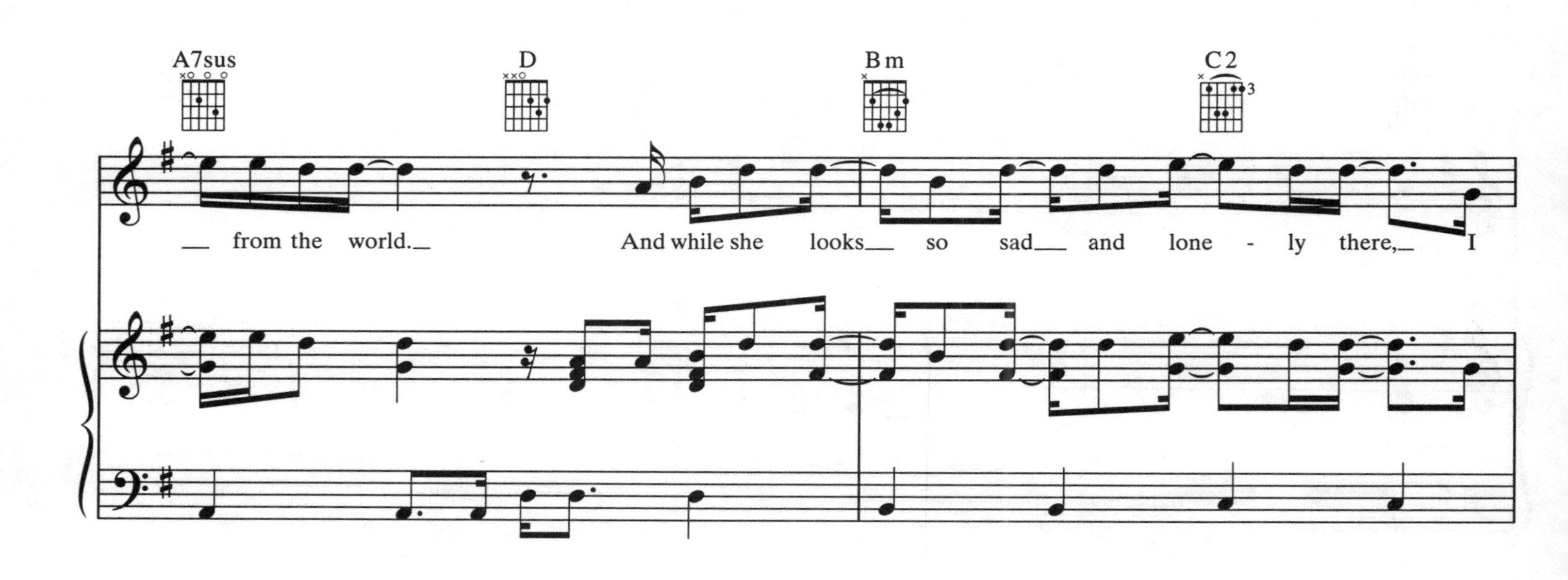
A7sus
D
Bm
C2
from the world. And while she looks so sad and lone - ly there, I

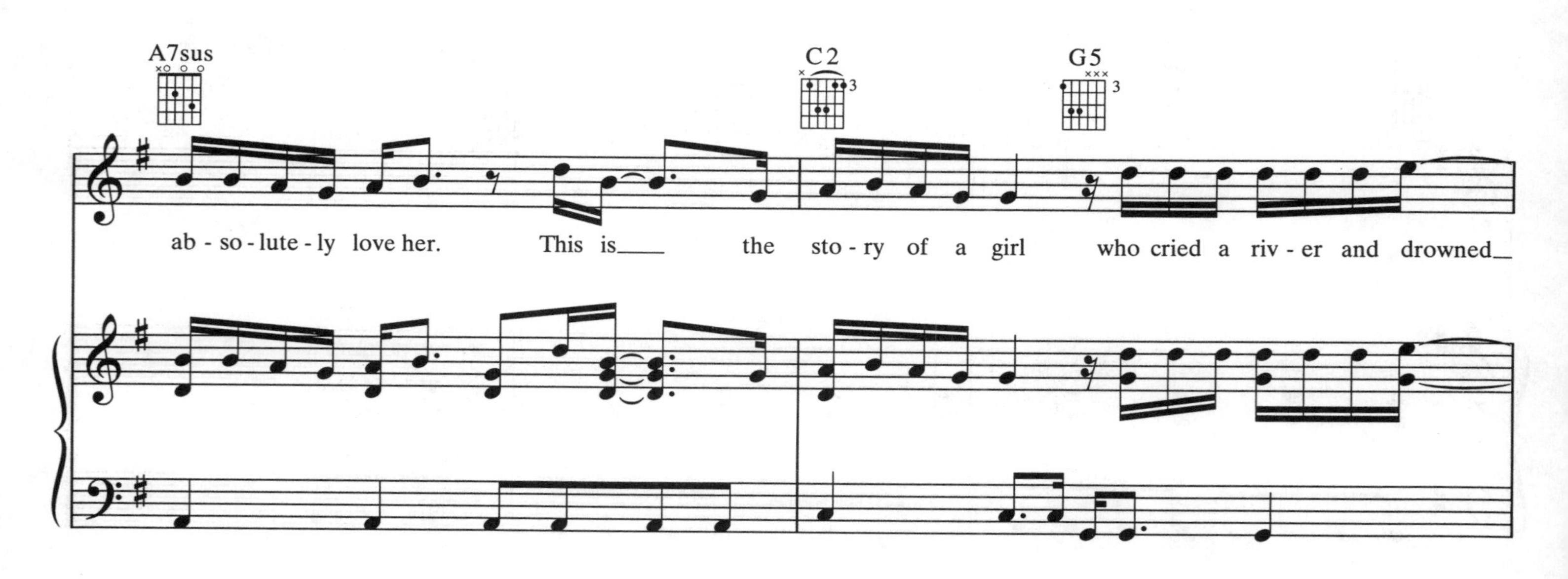
A7sus
C2
G5
ab - so - lute - ly love her. This is the sto - ry of a girl who cried a riv - er and drowned

A7sus
D
Bm
C2
3
the whole world. And while she looks so sad in pho - to - graphs, I
A7sus
N.C.
G
D
C
ab - so - lute - ly love her when she smiles,
G
D
C
G
D
C
G
when she smiles.

PRICE TO PLAY

Gtr. tuned
⑥ = G♭ ③ = D♭
⑤ = D♭ ② = G♭
④ = A♭ ① = B♭

Music by MICHAEL MUSHOK, AARON LEWIS,
JOHN APRIL and JONATHAN WYSOCKI
Lyrics by AARON LEWIS

Heavy rock ♩ = 112

* C♯5 B5 C♯5 B5 C♯5 B5 C♯5 B5 C♯5 B5 N.C.

f

C♯5 B5 C♯5 B5 C♯5 B5

1. C♯5 B5 C♯5 B5 E5

2. C♯5 B5 C♯5 B5 E5

Verse:
C♯5 B5 C♯5 B5 C♯5 B5

1.We fail to see
2. Ap - a - thy,

mf

*Chord frames reflect Mike Mushok's guitar tuning for this song.

C♯5 B5 C♯5 B5 N.C. C♯5 B5 C♯5 B5 C♯5 B5
how des - truc - tive we can be.
the cho - sen way to be.
C♯5 B5 C♯5 B5 E5 C♯5 B5 C♯5 B5 C♯5 B5
Tak - ing with - out giv -
Blind - ly look the oth -
C♯5 B5 C♯5 B5 N.C. C♯5 B5 C♯5 B5 C♯5 B5
ing back 'til the dam - age can be seen.
er way, while you waste a - way with me.
Pre-chorus:
C♯5 B5 C♯5 B5 E5 C♯5 B5 C♯5 B5 C♯5 B5
Can you see?
f

C♯5 B5 C♯5 B5 E5 C♯5 B5 C♯5 B5 C♯5 B5
Can you see?
C♯5 B5 C♯5 B5 Csus2
Chorus:
Asus2
The more you take,
Bsus2
the more you blame,
C♯sus2
but ev - 'ry - thing
C♯m
still feels the same.
Asus2
The more you hurt,

Bsus2
10
C♯sus2
12
the more you strain. The price you pay
C♯m
12
Asus2
8
to play the game. And all you seek,
Bsus2
10
C♯sus2
12
and all you gain, and all you step
C♯m
12
Asus2
8
on with no shame. There are no rules,

Bsus2
C♯sus2
no one, to blame, the price to play
1.
C♯m
C♯5
B5
the game.
N.C.
2.
Bridge:
What you pay to play the game.

C♯5
B5
What you pay to play the game.
C♯5
B5
What you pay to play the game.
1.
C♯5
D.S.𝄋
Bsus2
What you pay to play the game.
2.
C♯5
Bsus2
What you pay to play the game.

THE RED

Gtr. tuned down 1 1/2 steps:
⑥ = C♯ ③ = E
⑤ = F♯ ② = G♯
④ = B ① = C♯

Lyrics by PETE LOEFFLER
Music by CHEVELLE

E5
G5
E5
C5
C#5
E5
C#5
A5
The
the
red,
truth,
well, it
he gives
fil - ters
in - to
through.
most.
…end solo)
So lay
Chorus:
down.
The
threat
is

D5
B5
real,
when his
E5
C♯5
G5
E5
sight
goes
red a -
D5
B5
A5
F♯5
B5
G♯5
To Coda
1.
gain.
E5
C♯5
G5
E5
E5
C♯5
C5
A5
See - ing red a - gain.
mf

E5
G5
E5
C5
C♯5
E5
C♯5
A5
See - ing red a - gain.
2. This
Verse:
change,
He won't con - tain
Slip a -
way
to clear your mind.

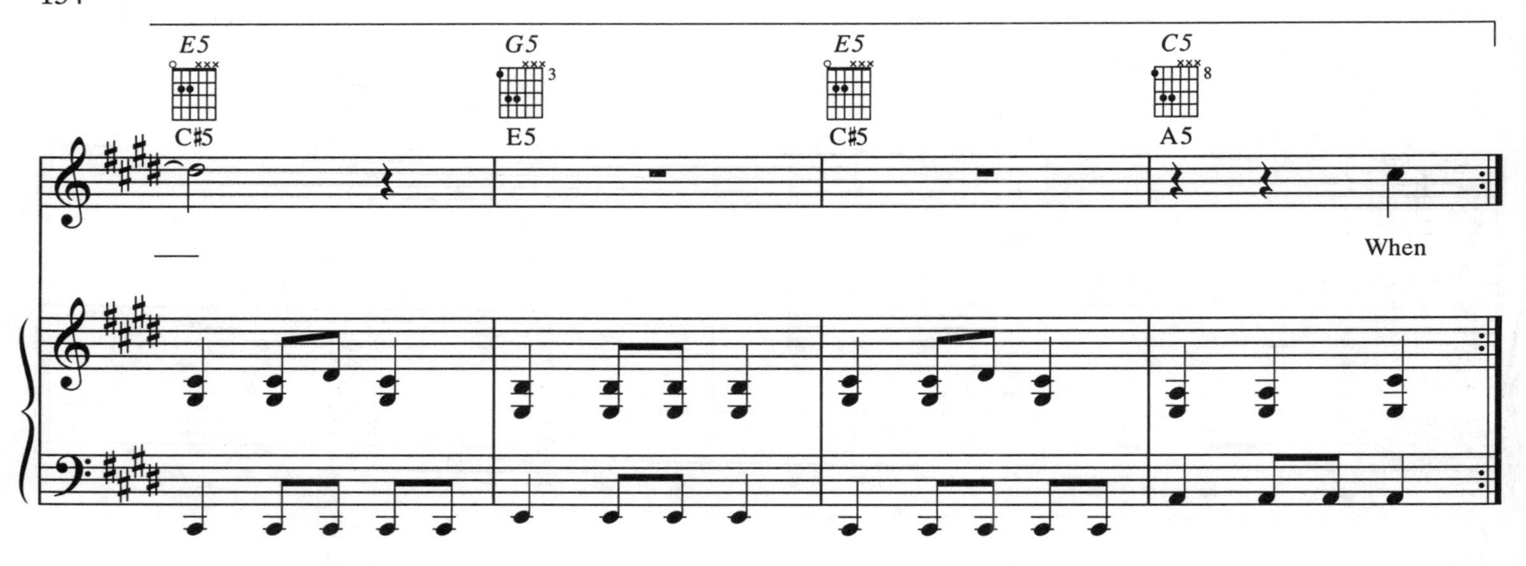
E5
G5
E5
C5
C♯5
E5
C♯5
A5
When

2.
D.S. al Coda
Coda
E5
G5
C♯5
E5
See - ing
red
a - gain.

1.2.3.
4.
E5
C5
C5
C♯5
A5
A5
See - ing
red
a - gain.
red.

A little slower ♩= 130
B5
G♯5
E5
C♯5
They say freak
mf
G5
E5
E5
C♯5
C5
A5
when you're sin - gled out.
The red,
rit.
it fil - ters through.

THE REASON

Words and Music by
DANIEL ESTRIN and
DOUGLAS ROBB

E
C♯m
A(9)
B
But I con - tin - ue learn - ing.
And all the pain I put you through,
3. I'm not a per - fect per - son.
I nev - er meant to do those things to you.
I wish that I could take it all a - way.
I nev - er meant to do those things to you.
And so, I have to say be - fore I go,
And be the one who catch - es all your tears.
And so, I have to say be - fore I go,
that I just want you to know
That's why I need you to hear.
that I just want you to know

Chorus:
E
I've found a rea - son for me
C♯m
to change who I used to be.
A2
To Coda
A rea - son to start o - ver
1.
B
new,
and the rea - son is

2.
B
new,
and the rea - son is
Bridge:
D
E
you,
(you,
and the rea - son is
is
you.
you,
And the rea - son is
is
D
you,
you,
E
D.S.𝄋 al Coda
and the rea - son is
is)
you.

Coda
B
new,
and the rea - son is
E
you.
C#m
I've found a rea - son to show
a
side of me you did-n't know,
A2
a rea - son for all that I
B
do,
and the rea - son is
rit.
E
you.

RIGHT HERE

Gtr. tuned down 1/2 step:
⑥ = E♭ ③ = G♭
⑤ = A♭ ② = B♭
④ = D♭ ① = E♭

Words and Music by
AARON LEWIS, MICHAEL MUSHOK,
JONATHAN WYSOCKI and JOHN APRIL

*This arrangement includes suggested guitar chords in standard tuning. The original guitar part was played on a baritone guitar tuned ⑥ = A♭, ⑤ = E♭, ④ = A♭, ③ = D♭, ② = E♭, ① = A♭. The complete authentic guitar-tab edition also is available from Alfred Publishing Co., Inc.

G6
G♭6
F♯7sus
F7sus
Asus2
A♭sus2
just give me a break and see the chang - es that I've made.
be so con - de - scend - ing, it's as much as I can take.
Bsus
B♭sus
I've
And
Asus2
A♭sus2
got some im - per - fec - tions, but how can you col - lect
you're so in - de - pen - dent, you just re - fuse to bend,
G6
G♭6
F♯7sus
F7sus
Asus2
A♭sus2
them all and throw them in my face?
so I keep bend - ing till I break.

Chorus:
Dsus2
D♭sus2
F♯m7
Fm7
B7sus
B♭7sus
But you al - ways find a way to keep me right
G6/9
G♭6/9
here wait - ing. You al - ways find the words to say
to keep me right here wait - ing.
(1.2.) And if you chose
(3.) And if I chose

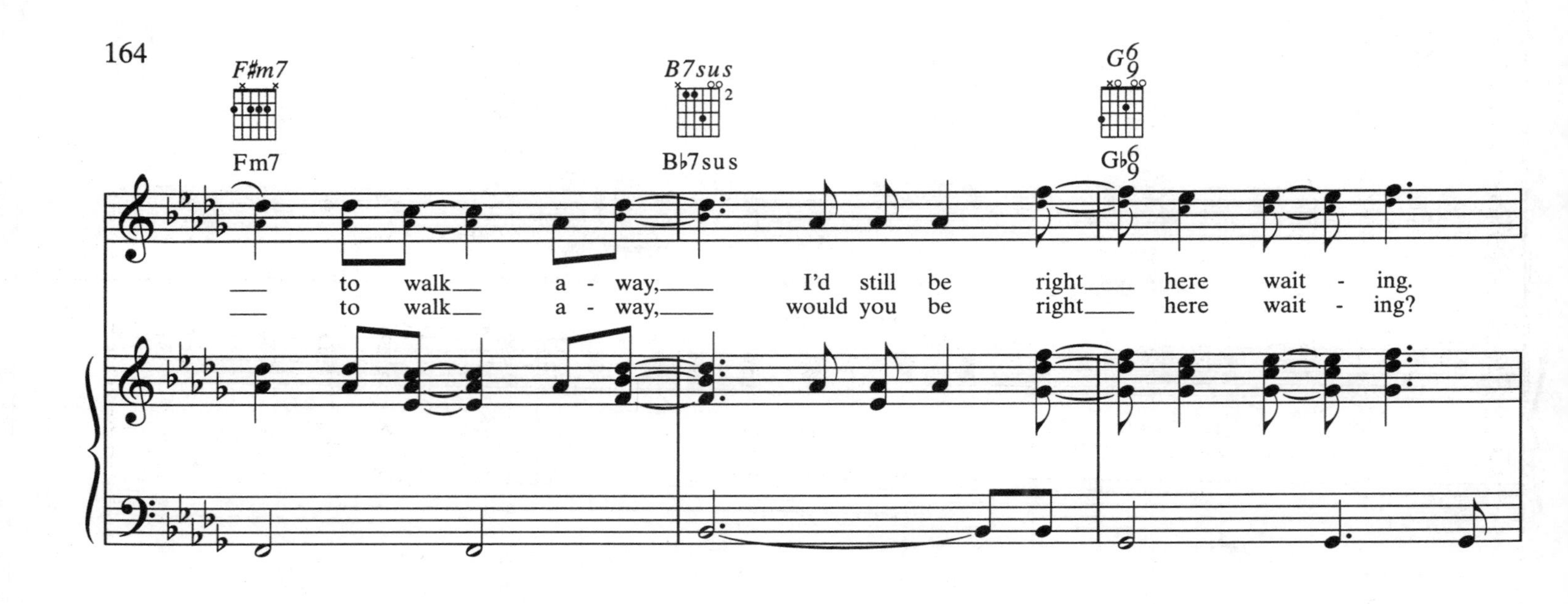
F#m7
B7sus
G6/9
Fm7
B♭7sus
G♭6/9
to walk a - way, I'd still be right here wait - ing.
to walk a - way, would you be right here wait - ing?

Dsus2
F#m7
B7sus
To Coda
D♭sus2
Fm7
B♭7sus
Search-ing for the things to say to keep you right
Search-ing for the things to say to keep me right

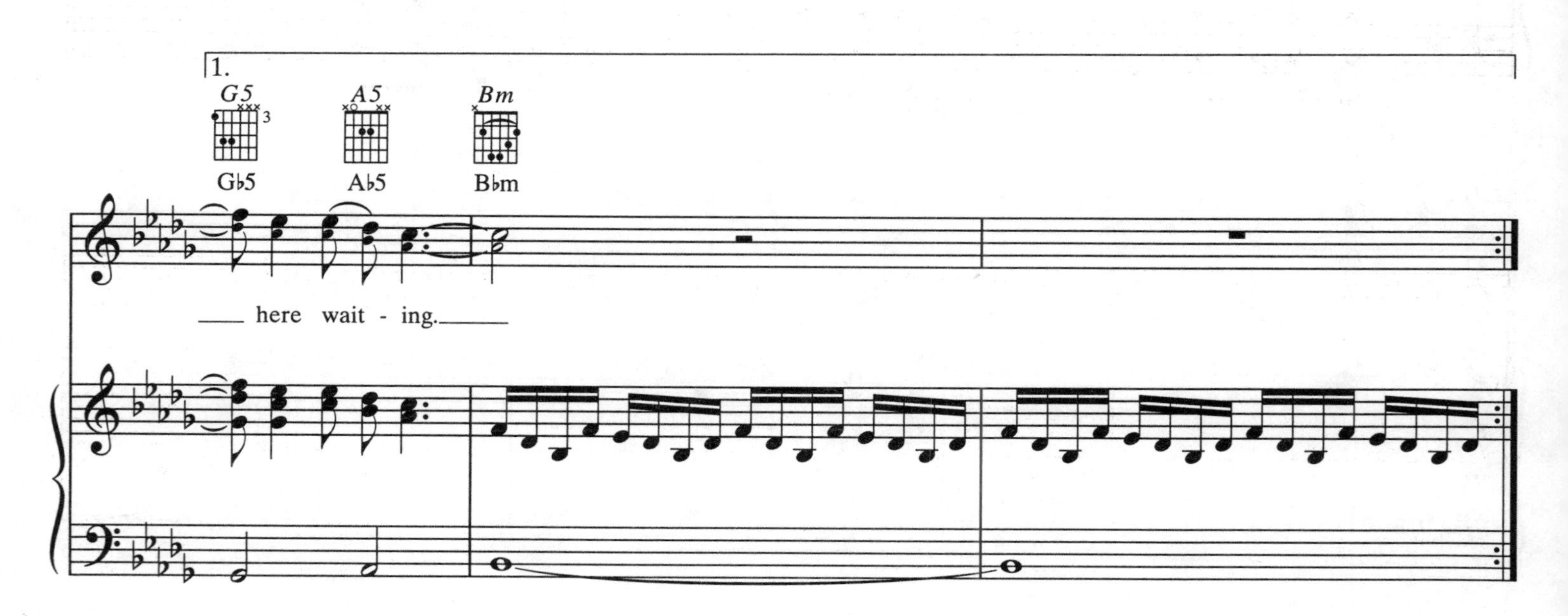
1.
G5
A5
Bm
G♭5
A♭5
B♭m
here wait - ing.

2.
Bridge:
G5 A5 B5 G5 B5 G5
G♭5 A♭5 B♭5 G♭5 B♭5 G♭5
here wait - ing.
I've made a com - mit - ment.
B5 G5 B5 G5 B5 G5
B♭5 G♭5 B♭5 G♭5 B♭5 G♭5
I'm will - ing to bleed for you.
I
B5 G5 B5 G5 B5 G5
B♭5 G♭5 B♭5 G♭5 B♭5 G♭5
need - ed ful - fill - ment.
I found what I need in you.
Verse 3:
Bsus
B♭sus
Asus2
A♭sus2
3. Why can't you just for - give me?
I

G6
Gb6
don't want to re - live all the mis - takes
F#7sus
F7sus
Asus2
Absus2
Bsus
Bbsus
I've made a - long the way.
Chorus:
D6sus2
Db6sus2
But I al - ways find a way to keep you right
here wait - ing. I al - ways find the words to say

Bsus
G6
D.S. 𝄋 al Coda
B♭sus
G♭6
to keep you right here wait - ing.
Coda
G5
A5
Bm
G♭5
A♭5
B♭m
here wait - ing.

SOMEDAY

Lyrics by CHAD KROEGER,
MIKE KROEGER and RYAN PEAKE
Music by NICKELBACK

Bm
G2
A2
D2
Late - ly there's been too much of this, but don't think it's too late.
Let's re - write an end - ing that fits, in stead of a Hol-ly-wood hor - ror.
E5
A5
N.C.
Noth - ing's wrong, just as long as you know that some - day I will...
Chorus:
G(9)
D
A2
Em
Some - day, some - how, I'm gon - na make it al - right, but not right now.
G(9)
A2
Bm
Asus
A
I know you're won - der - ing when.
(You're the on - ly one who knows that.)

G(9)
D
A2
Em
Some - day,___ some - how,___ I'm gon-na make it al - right,_ but not right now._
G(9)
A2
To Coda
1.
Bm
I know you're won - der - ing when.___
2. Well, I'd
2.
Bm
G(9)
D
(You're the on - ly one who knows that.___)
A2
Em
G(9)
A2
Bm
A

G(9)
D
A2
Em
G(9)
A2
Bm
D.S. 𝄋 al Coda
Coda
Bm
A2
(You're the on - ly one who knows that.)
G(9)
A2
Bm
A2
I know you're won-der - ing when.
(You're the on - ly one who knows_ that.)
G(9)
A2
Bm7/E
I know you're won-der - ing when.
rit.

TOO BAD

Lyrics by
CHAD KROEGER

Music by
NICKELBACK

Dm
Cm
Dm/F
Cm/E♭
fe on Main Street, with mouths to feed,
G2
F2
Dm
Cm
just try'n' to keep cloth - ing on our backs. And all I hear
Dm/C
Cm/B♭
1. 2.
To Next Strain
G2
F2
a - bout is how it's so bad, so bad. It's too bad
3.
G5
F5
Dm
Cm
... end solo)

4.
G2
F2
and how it's so bad, it's so bad, it's so bad, it's so bad. It's too bad,
Chorus:
Bb5
Ab5
F
Eb
Gm7
Fm7
it's stu - pid, too late, so wrong, so long.
G5
F5
Bb5
Ab5
F
Eb
It's too bad we had no time to re - wind; let's walk, let's talk.
Gm7
Fm7
1.
G5
F5
Dm
Cm
Dm/F
Cm/Eb
Let's talk.

Verse 2:
You left without saying goodbye,
Although I'm sure you tried.
You call the house from time to time
To make sure we're alive.
But you weren't there
Right when I needed you the most.
And now I dream about it,
And how it's so bad, it's so bad.
(To Chorus:)

Verse 4:
Father's hands are lined with guilt
From tearing us apart.
Guess it turned out in the end;
Just look at where we are.
We made it out;
We still got clothing on our backs.
And now I scream about it,
And how it's so bad, it's so bad,
It's so bad, it's so bad.
(To Chorus:)

SHUT UP!

Gtr. tuned down 1/2 step:
⑥ = E♭ ③ = G♭
⑤ = A♭ ② = B♭
④ = D♭ ① = E♭

Words and Music by
SIMPLE PLAN

A5
Ab5
G5
Gb5
A5
Ab5
D5
Db5
show, it's all a - bout you. You think you know what ev - 'ry - one
lie, what - ev - er you do. You think you're spe - cial, but I know,
G5
Gb5
A5
Ab5
G5
Gb5
A5
Ab5
needs. You al - ways take time to crit - i - cize me. It seems like
and I know, and I know, and we know that you're not. You're al - ways
B5
Bb5
A5
Ab5
G5
Gb5
ev - 'ry - day I make mis - takes, I just can't get it right.
there to point out my mis - takes and shove them in my face.
A5
Ab5
D5
Db5
B5
Bb5
A5
Ab5
It's like I'm the one you love to hate but

Chorus:
G5
G♭5
A5
A♭5
D5
D♭5
not to - day.
So, shut up, shut up, shut up,
A5
A♭5
B5
B♭5
G5
G♭5
A5
A♭5
don't wan - na hear it. Get out, get out, get out, get out of my way.
D5
D♭5
A5
A♭5
B5
B♭5
Step up, step up, step up, you'll nev - er stop me. Noth - ing you say to - day
G5
G♭5
A5
A♭5
1.
D5
D♭5
A5
A♭5
G5
G♭5
is gon - na bring me down.

A5
D5
Ab5
Db5
A5
G5
Ab5
Gb5
A5
Ab5
2. There you
2.
D5
Db5
down.
G5
Gb5
Shut up, shut up, shut up,
A5
D5
Ab5
Db5
is gon - na bring me down.

Half time ♩= 78
G5
Gb5
Asus
Absus
D5
Db5
Asus
Absus
Shut up, shut up, shut up, you'll nev - er bring me down.
G2
Gb2
Asus
Absus
D5
Db5
Asus
Absus
G2
Gb2
Asus
Absus
Bridge:
D5
Db5
Asus
Absus
G2
Gb2
Asus
Absus
D5
Db5
Asus
Absus
Don't tell me who I should be and don't try to tell me what's right
(Don't tell me who I should be.)
G2
Gb2
Asus
Absus
D5
Db5
Asus
Absus
G2
Gb2
Asus
Absus
for me. Don't tell me what I should do. I don't wan-na

Double time ♩= 156
Chorus:
D5 A5 G5 D5
D♭5 A♭5 G♭5 D♭5
waste my time or watch you fade a - way.
So, shut up, shut up, shut up,
down.
A5 B5 G5 A5
A♭5 B♭5 G♭5 A♭5
don't wan - na hear it. Get out, get out, get out, get out of my way.
D5 A5 B5
D♭5 A♭5 B♭5
1.
Step up, step up, step up, you'll nev - er stop me. Noth - ing you say to - day
G5 A5 B5
G♭5 A♭5 B♭5
2.
N.C.
is gon - na bring me Noth - ing you say is gon - na bring me

Half-time feel
D5
Db5
A5
Ab5
G5
Gb5
down.
Bring me down.
Shut up, shut up, shut up.
A5
Ab5
D5
Db5
A5
Ab5
You won't bring me down,
bring me
G5
Gb5
A5
Ab5
G5
Gb5
N.C.
down.
Shut up, shut up, shut up.
You won't bring me...
Shut up, shut up, shut up!

TOO LITTLE TOO LATE

Words and Music by
STEVEN PAGE and ED ROBERTSON

C2/G
D2/A
G5
A5
'ry - thing I do con - found you?" You say
G/B
A/C#
C
D
G/B
A/C#
that I pulled the world from un - der you, you can't
A
B
go through it this time. And I could be
Chorus:
G
A
D
E
F
G
C
D
D
E
good, and I would if I knew I was un - der - stood. And it - 'll be

G
A
D
E
F
G
C
D
G5
A5
great, just wait, or is it too lit - tle too late? Whoo!
G
A
C2/G
D/A
G5
A5
Verse 2:
G/B
A/C♯
C2
D2
2. One day this em - bar - rass - ment will fade
G
A
G/B
A/C♯
be - hind me, and that day I could think
(2nd time - Inst. solo ad lib....

C2
D2
G5
A5
of things that won't re - mind me.
But these days
G/B
A/C♯
C
D
G/B
A/C♯
it's un - bear - a - ble for both of us, we can't
A
B
B
C♯
dis - cuss it this way, this way.
...end solo)
Bridge:
Em
F♯m
D
E
G
A
A
B
I'm gain - ing strength, trying to learn to pull my own
Re - cord and play, af - ter years of end - less re -

Em
F♯m
D/F♯
E/G♯
weight. I'm gain - ing pounds at the pre -
wind. Yes - ter - day wasn't half
To Coda
G
A
B
C♯
ci - pice of too late, just wait. I could be
as tough as this
Chorus:
D
E
F
C
good, and I would if I knew I was un - der -
D.S. al Coda
stood. And it - 'll be great, just wait, or is it too lit - tle too late?

Coda
A
B
G/B
A/C♯
C2
D2
D
E
Em
F♯m
time. This time is-n't Hell, last time I could-n't tell,
mf
D/F♯
E/G♯
G
A
A
B
B
C♯
this mind was-n't well, next time, hope
Chorus:
G
A
D
E
F
G
C
D
I'm going to be good, and I would if I knew I was un-der-
cresc.
f
stood. And it-'ll be great, just wait, or is it too lit-tle too late? Good,

D F C D
E G D E
and I would if I knew I was un - der - stood. And it - 'll be
G D F C G5
A E G D A5
great, just wait, or is it too lit - tle too late?
G C2/G G5
A D2/A A5
G C2/G
A D2/A
G5
A5
f

Gtr. tuned down 1/2 step:
⑥ = E♭ ③ = G♭
⑤ = A♭ ② = B♭
④ = D♭ ① = E♭

SO FAR AWAY

Music and Lyrics by
AARON LEWIS

G D C(9) D
Gb Db Cb(9) Db
I, I must be sleep - ing.
Chorus:
G D Em7
Gb Db Ebm7
Now that we're here, it's so far a - way all the
C(9) G D
Cb(9) Gb Db
strug-gle we thought was in vain. All the mis-takes, one life con-tained.
Em7 C(9) G
Ebm7 Cb(9) Gb
They all fi - n'lly start to go a - way. Now that we're here

D Em7 C(9)
D♭ E♭m7 C♭(9)
it's so far a - way and I feel like I can face the day.
G D Em7
G♭ D♭ E♭m7
I can for - give, and I'm not a - shamed to be the
C(9)
C♭(9)
To Coda
1. 2.
per - son that I am to - day. 2. These are my
Bridge:
Em9 D/F# G D/A
E♭m9 D♭/F G♭ D♭/A♭
I'm so a - fraid of wak - ing.

Cmaj7
D
Em9
D/F#
Em9
D/F#
Cbmaj7
Db
Ebm9
Db/F
Ebm9
Db/F
Please don't shake me. I'm a-fraid of
D.S. % al Coda
G
D/A
Cmaj7
D
Em9
D/F#
Gb
Db/Ab
Cbmaj7
Db
Ebm9
Db/F
wak - ing. Please don't shake me.
Coda

UNTITLED
(How Can This Happen to Me?)

All gtrs. tune down 1/2 step*
⑥ = E♭ ③ = G♭
⑤ = A♭ ② = B♭
④ = D♭ ① = E♭

Words and Music by
SIMPLE PLAN

Moderately slow ♩ = 90

G

mp

(with pedal)

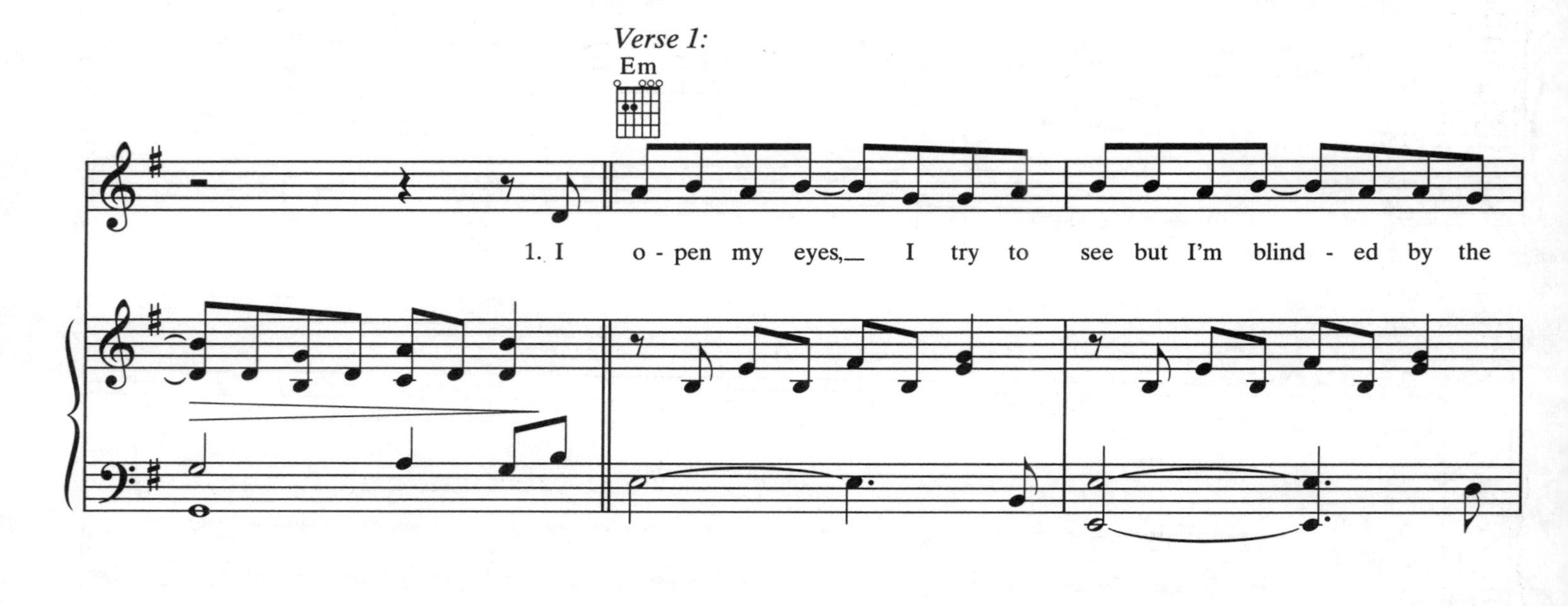

*Recorded in F♯ major.

G
D
mem-ber why.__ I'm ly-ing here__ to-night__ and I
C
D
Em
can't stand__ the pain.__ And I can't make_ it go_
G
C
D
__ a-way.__ No, I can't stand__ the pain.__
Chorus:
Dsus
D
G
Em
How could this hap-pen to me?__ I've made my mis-takes,__ got no-where to run._
mf

C
D6
G
The night goes on as I'm fad - ing a - way.
I'm sick of this life,
Em
C
D6
To Coda
I just wan - na scream.
How could this hap - pen to me?
G
Verse 2:
Em
2. Ev - 'ry - bod - y's scream-ing, I
G
try to make a sound but no one hears me.
I'm

Em
G
slip-ping off the edge, I'm hang-ing by a thread. I wan-na start this o-ver a-gain.
D
C
D
So, I try to hold on to a
Em
G
C
time when noth-ing mat-tered and I can't ex-plain
D
Em
G
what hap-pened. And I can't e-rase the things that I've done.

C
D
No I can't.
Dsus
D
D.S. 𝄋 al Coda
How could this hap - pen to me?
Coda
C
D5
(Gtr. solo ad lib....
Em
G
C
D

Em7
...end solo)
Chorus:
G
Em
C
I've made my mis - takes,
got no-where to run.
The night goes on
D6
G
Em
as I'm fad - ing a - way.
I'm sick of this life,
I just wan-na scream.
C
D6
C(9)
How could this hap - pen to me?

WELCOME TO MY LIFE

Words and Music by
SIMPLE PLAN

Am
Fmaj7
B♭m
G♭maj7
lock your-self__ in your room__ with the ra - di - o on, turned up so loud__ that
sick of ev - 'ry-one a - round__ with the big fake smiles and stu - pid lies__ while
G5
Fmaj7
A♭5
G♭maj7
no one hears you scream - ing?
deep in - side, you're bleed - ing?
No, you don't know what it's like__ when
Am7
Fmaj7
B♭m7
G♭maj7
noth-ing feels__ al - right.
You don't know what it's like__ to be like
Chorus:
G5
C
Am7
Fmaj7
A♭5
D♭
B♭m7
G♭maj7
me.
To be hurt, to feel lost, to be

C
G5
C
Am7
Fmaj7
D♭
A♭5
D♭
B♭m7
G♭maj7
left out in the dark to be kicked when you're down, to feel like
you've been pushed a - round, to be on the edge of break - ing down when
To Coda
Dm7
C/E
E♭m7
D♭/F
no one's there to save you, No, you don't know what it's like.
1.
F5
G♭5
Wel - come to my life.
2. Do you

2.
F5
Gb5
C
Db
Wel - come to my life.
Bridge:
G5
Ab5
F5
Gb5
C5
Db5
No one ev - er lied straight to your face__ and
Am
Bbm
C5
Db5
F5
Gb5
G5
Ab5
no one ev - er stabbed you in the back._ You might think_ I'm hap - py, but I'm
C
Db
Gsus
Absus
F5
Gb5
C5
Db5
not gon-na be O K.____ Ev - 'ry-bod - y al-ways gave you what you want - ed. You

Am C5 D5 C/E
B♭m D♭5 E♭5 D♭/F
never had to work, it was always there. You don't know what it's like, what it's
F5 Am Fmaj7 C G5
G♭5 B♭m G♭maj7 D♭ A♭5
like to be hurt, to feel lost, to be left out in the dark, to be
Am Fmaj7 C G5 C
B♭m G♭maj7 D♭ A♭5 D♭
kicked when you're down, to feel like you've been pushed a - round, to be
Am7 Fmaj7 C G5
B♭m7 G♭maj7 D♭ A♭5
on the edge of break - ing down when no one's there to save you, No, you

D.S. 𝄋 al Coda
Dm7
C/E
F5
E♭m7
D♭/F
G♭5
don't know what it's like
to be
Coda
F5
G♭5
C
D♭
Wel - come to my life.
Am
B♭m
Fmaj7
G♭maj7
Wel - come to my life.
G5
A♭5
C
D♭
Wel - come to my life.

WHEN IT'S OVER

Words and Music by
MARK McGRATH, STAN FRAZIER, RODNEY SHEPPARD,
CRAIG BULLOCK and MATTHEW KARGES

Moderately ♩= 100

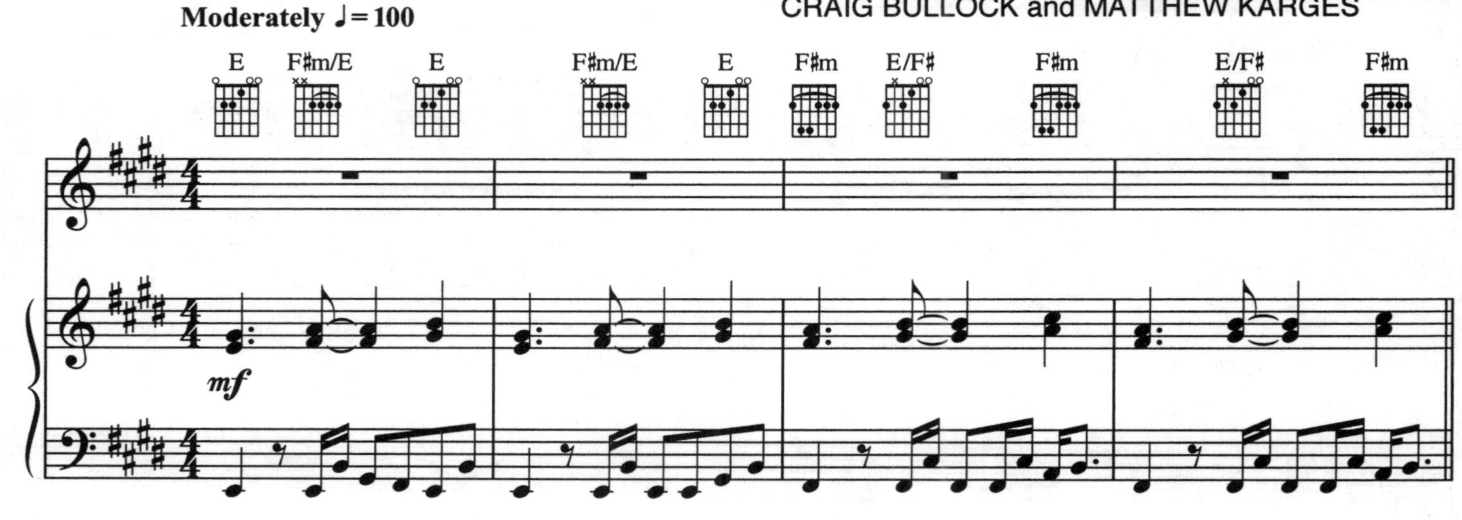

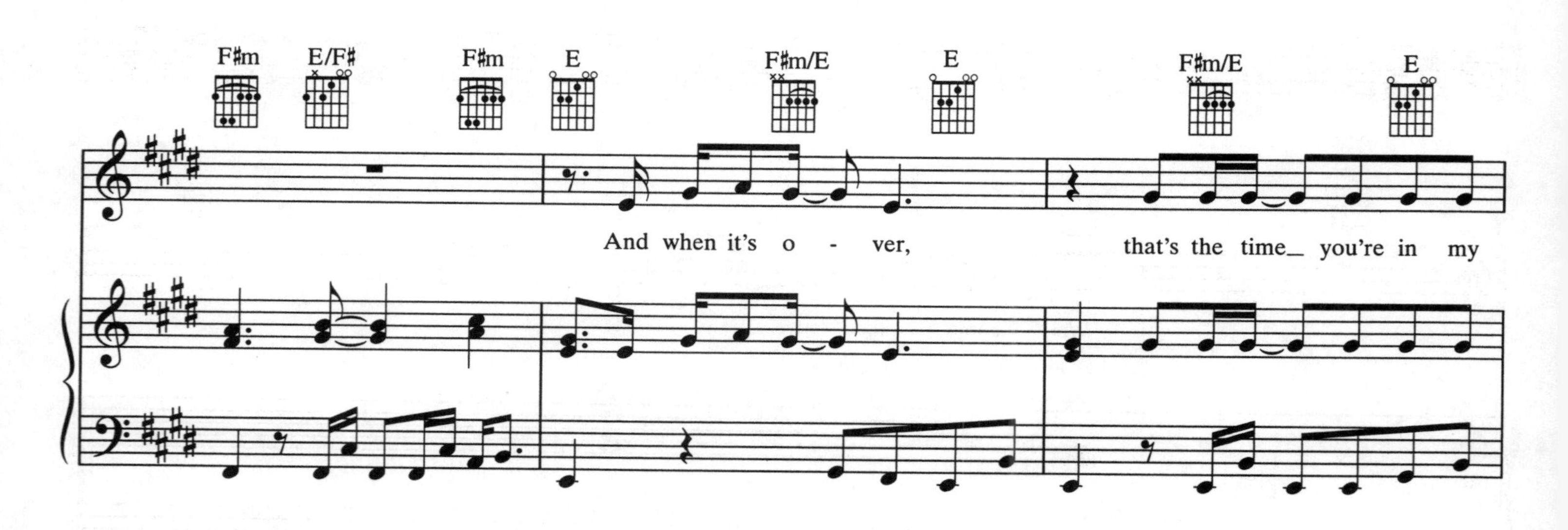

F♯m
E/F♯
E
F♯m/E
heart a - gain.
And when you go, go, go,
go, I know it nev - er ends, nev - er ends.
Chorus:
All the things that I used to say, all the words that got in the way,
all the things that I used to know have gone out the win - dow.

E
F♯m/E
E
F♯m/E
E
All the things that she used to bring,
all the songs that she used to sing,
F♯m
E/F♯
F♯m
E/F♯
F♯m
all the fav - 'rite T V shows have gone out the win - dow.
2. I'm miss - ing
3. I'm wish - ing
Verses 2 & 3:
E
F♯m/E
E
F♯m/E
E
you.
you,
I nev - er knew how much she loved
you nev - er said you were pre - tend -
F♯m
E/F♯
F♯m
E/F♯
F♯m
me.
ing.
I'm miss - ing
I'm wish - ing

E
F♯m/E
E
F♯m/E
E
you.
you,
I never knew how much you meant
you'd feel the same and just come back
to me.
to me.
F♯m
E/F♯
F♯m
E/F♯
F♯m
I need you. And when you
E
F♯m/E
E
F♯m/E
E
go, go, go, go, I know,
F♯m
E/F♯
F♯m
1.
E/F♯
F♯m
it never ends, never ends.

2.
Bridge:
E/F♯
F♯m
F♯m7
C♯m7
never ends. When it's over, can I still come over?
A
B/A
B
E/B
And when it's over,
is it really over?
A/B
E
N.C.
When it's over, that's the time I fall in love again.

Chorus:
E
F♯m/E
E
F♯m/E
E
All the things that I___ used to say,
all the words that got__ in the way,___
F♯m
E/F♯
F♯m
E/F♯
F♯m
all the things that I___ used to know have gone out the win - dow.
E
F♯m/E
E
F♯m/E
E
All the things that she__ used to bring,
all the songs that she__ used to sing,___
Repeat ad lib. and fade
F♯m
E/F♯
F♯m
E/F♯
F♯m
all the fav - 'rite T___ V shows__ have gone out the win - dow.

YOU'RE A GOD

Gtr. tuned down 1/2 step:
⑥ = E♭ ③ = G♭
⑤ = A♭ ② = B♭
④ = D♭ ① = E♭

Words and Music by
MATTHEW SCANNELL

G(9)
A
G(9)
G♭(9)
A♭
G♭(9)
Nev - er a - gain,
no,
no, nev - er a - gain.
Chorus:
A
B5
G♯m7
A♭
B♭5
Gm7
'Cause you're a god and I am not and
B/F♯
E2
B5
B♭/F
E♭2
B♭5
I just thought that you would know.
You're a god and
To Coda 1.
G♯m7
B/F♯
E2
Gm7
B♭/F
E♭2
I am not and I just thought I'd let you go.

2.
Bsus
Bbsus
E2
Eb2
let you go.
C#m
Cm
A
Ab
B5
Bb5
C#m
Cm
A
Ab
B5
Bb5
D.S. al Coda

Coda
E2
E♭2
B5
B♭5
G♯m7
Gm7
let you go.
You're a god
oh, and I am not.
B/F♯
B♭/F
E2
E♭2
B5
B♭5
I just thought that you would know.
You're a god
G♯m7
Gm7
B/F♯
B♭/F
E2
E♭2
oh, and I am not.
I just thought I'd let you go.
Repeat ad lib. and fade
Bsus
B♭sus
B
B♭
B2
B♭2
B
B♭

All gtrs. in Drop D, tuned down 1½ steps:
⑥ = B ③ = E
⑤ = F♯ ② = G
④ = B ① = C♯

VITAMIN R (LEADING US ALONG)

Words by PETE LOEFFLER
Music by CHEVELLE

Slowly ♩. = 63

D2 B2 D5 B5

mf

D2 B2 D5 B5

Verse:

Dm Bm D2 B2

1. Some will learn, man - y do
2. *See additional lyrics*

Dm
Bm
D2
B2
cov - er up
or
spread it
Bb5
G5
Bb5(#11)
G5(#11)
out.
Turn a - round,
had e - nough.
Bb5
G5
Bb5(#11)
G5(#11)
Pick and choose
or
pass it
Dm
Bm
D2
B2
on.
Buy - ing in,
head - ing for

Dm
Bm
D2
B2
suf - fer now or suf - fer
Bb5
G5
Bb5(#11)
G5(#11)
then. It's bad e - nough, I want the fear,
Bb5
G5
Bb5(#11)
G5(#11)
need the fear, 'cause he's a -
Dm
Bm
lone.
(He has be -

F
D
come.
He's a -
Dm
Bm
lone.
(He has be -
G
E
come.
F
D
Well, if they're
Chorus:
B♭5
G5
mak - ing it, then they're push - ing it, and they're
(Mak - ing it.) (Push - ing it.)
C5
A5

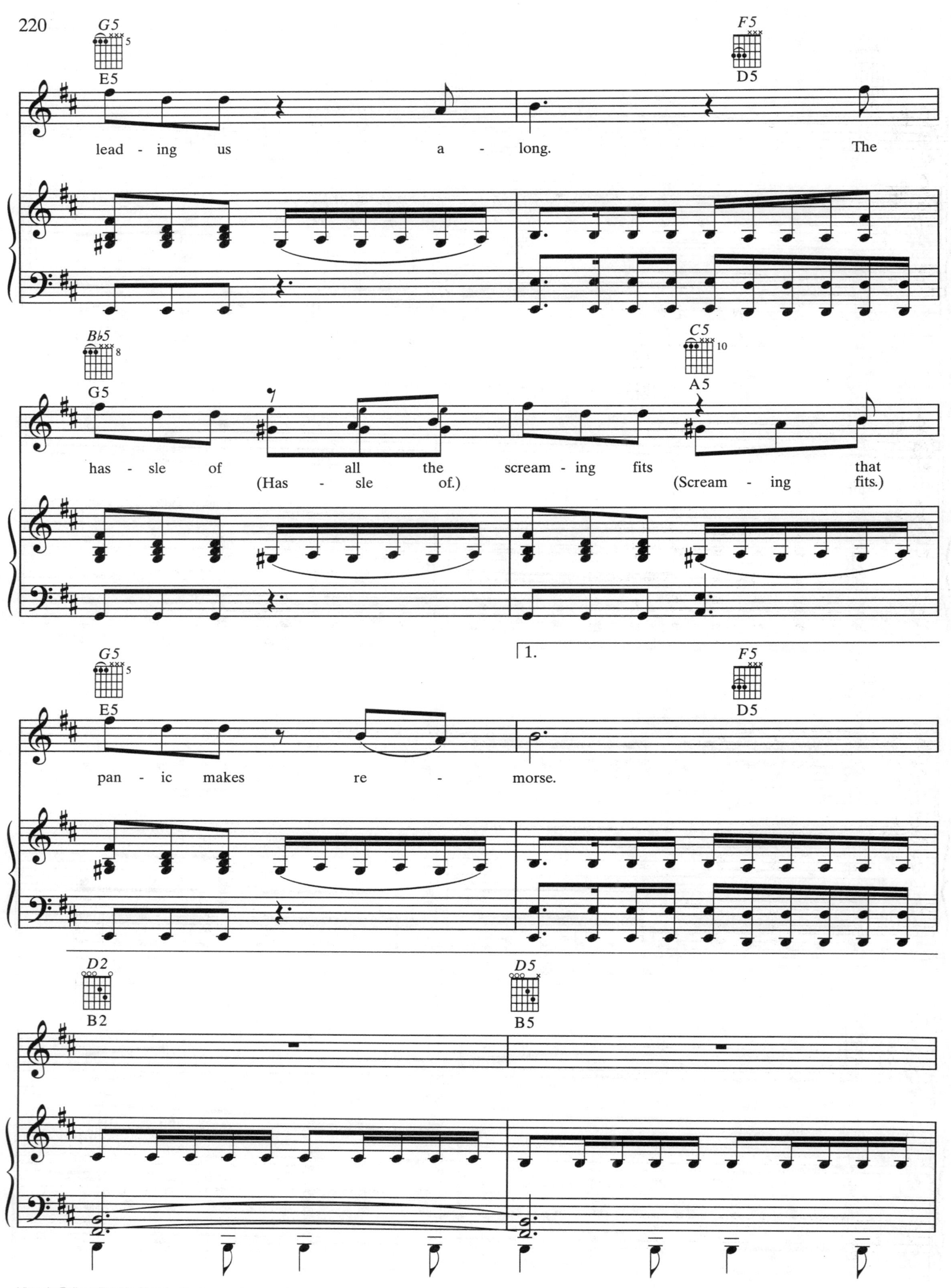
G5
E5
F5
D5
lead - ing us a - long. The
Bb5
G5
C5
A5
has - sle of all the scream - ing fits that
(Has - sle of.) (Scream - ing fits.)
G5
E5
1.
F5
D5
pan - ic makes re - morse.
D2
B2
D5
B5

D2
B2
D5
B5
2.
Bridge:
F5
D5
F5
D5
D5
B5
morse.
O - ver and
G5
E5
D5
B5
o - ver a slave
B♭5
G5
F5
D5
be - came. O - ver and

G5
E5
D5
B5
o - ver a slave
B♭5
G5
F5
D5
be - came. O - ver and
G5
E5
D5
B5
D2
B2
o - ver a slave.
D5
B5
D2
B2

D5
B5
Bb5
G5
8
Well, if they're mak - ing it, then they're
(Mak - ing it.
C5
A5
10
G5
E5
5
push - ing it, and they're lead - ing us a -
(Push - ing it.)
F5
D5
Bb5
G5
8
long. The has - sle of all the
(Has - sle of.)
2. Like a can - cer caused all the
(Can - cer caused.)
C5
A5
10
G5
E5
5
scream - ing fits that pan - ic held be -
(Scream - ing fits.)
scream - ing fits and their pan - ic makes re -

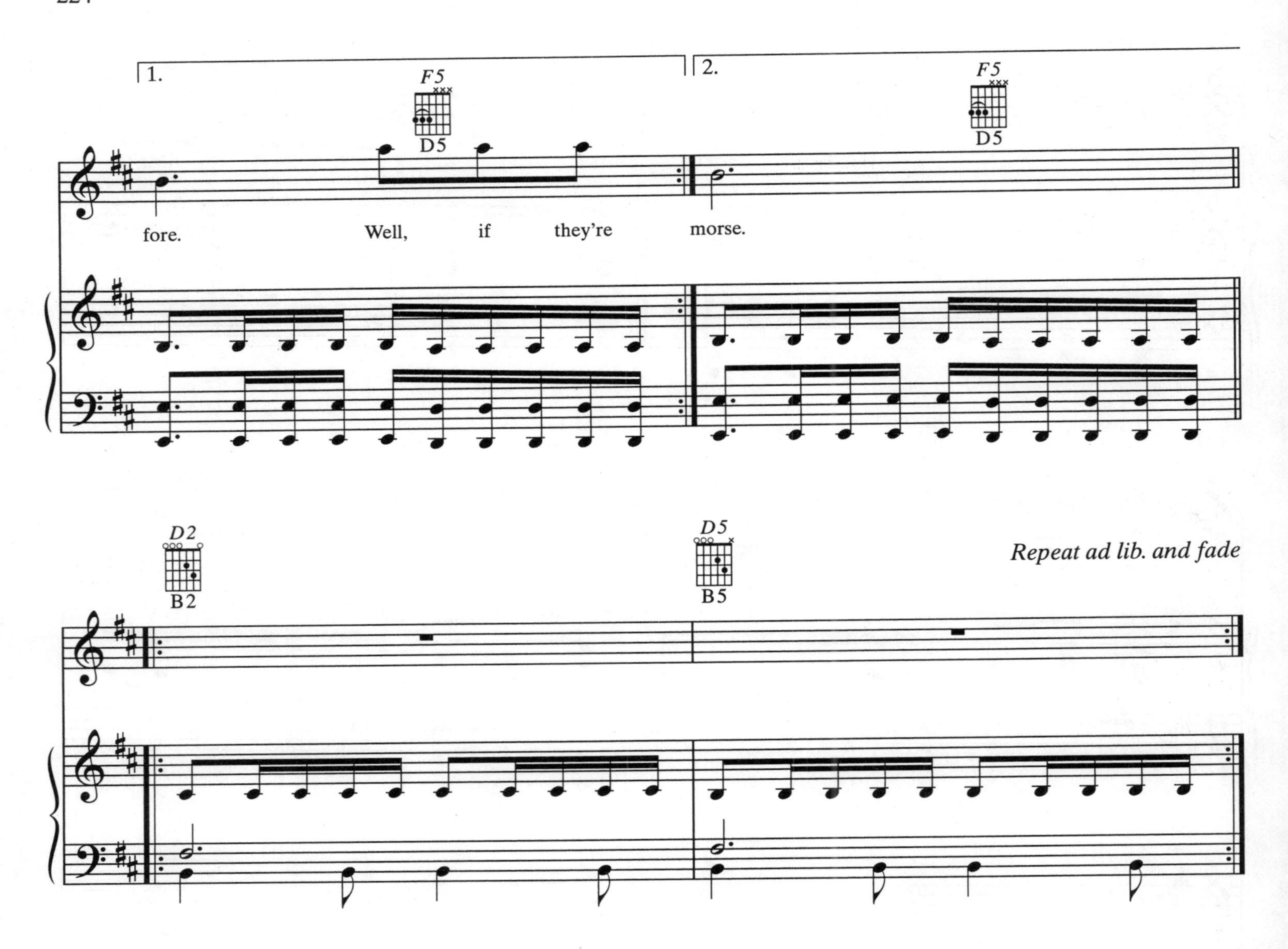

Verse 2:
After all, what's the point?
Course levitation is possible
If you're a fly, achieved and gone,
There's time for this and so much more.
It's typical, create a world,
A special place of my design.
To never cope or never care,
Just use the key 'cause he's alone.
(To Pre-chorus:)